LAND & ARCHAEOLOGY

Histories of Human Environment
in the British Isles

John G. Evans

First published in 1999 by Tempus Publishing Ltd

Reprinted in 2010 by
The History Press
The Mill, Brimscombe Port,
Stroud, Gloucestershire, GL5 2QG
www.thehistorypress.co.uk

British Library Cataloguing in Publication Data.
A catalogue record for this book is available from the British Library.

ISBN 978 0 7524 1463 8

Typesetting and origination by Tempus Publishing.
Printed and bound in England

Contents

Dedication

For Vivian and Jodi

Preface

Phenomenology . . . traces the *a priori* connections between concepts whose role is not to explain the world, but to focus our emotions upon it. It describes the way the world appears to us; and shows how appearances matter.

Roger Scruton 1996, *An intelligent person's guide to philosophy*

This book is about histories of human environment in the British Isles from the earliest known people to the Middle Ages. To this extent, it is similar to *The environment of early man in the British Isles* which I wrote in 1975, but there are new approaches which take on board changing ideas in the last quarter-century. Especially, the book seeks to explore environments at a small scale rather than in broad period-based and regional schemes.

'Human' refers to the species of *Homo* — *H. heidelbergensis, H. sapiens neanderthalensis* and *H. sapiens sapiens*. All had similar mental facilities, particularly the ability to plan knowingly and for purposeful goals. 'Environment' refers to the biophysical surrounds, how these were used in the every day business of life as well as in a more spiritual role.

But neither people nor environments existed on their own. People interpreted their thoughts and actions, stimuli from other people and environments variously and behaved accordingly. They changed the environment in their minds and physically, and in doing so were changed themselves. These interactions mediated relationships between people and eased their way in life; this I have referred to, after sociological usage, as 'the expressive order'. In biology, relationships between organisms and environments are understood in the concept of 'niche'. For humans, a better word is 'locality', again following the sociologists, and especially the writings of Peter Dickens, because this takes on board the concept of expressiveness: localities can be constituted, used and dispersed quite rapidly. A 'locality' is an abstraction, a reflexive articulation of people and environment - in Dickens' definition, 'a local social system'. I *never* use it in a sense of concrete architecture. 'Locale', on the other hand, is used in just this way. 'Location' is a more general term which means the positioning of a thing or activity in the physical environment.

The book has been written roughly chronologically because history is cumulative; you cannot understand any present outside its past. But it is not a single history. Without comparisons between regions or with other continental archipelagoes or the adjacent continent, no single history of these islands can be written. Nor are there broad schemes of change or progression because although you can recognise these in climate or culture you cannot recognise relationships between the two on a country-wide scale. So there is no Atlantic period or Middle Bronze Age in this book, and I have used other broad names like the Roman period largely as landmarks. I am not saying that broad spatial and temporal schemes do not exist, and one day it may be possible to identify them and use them in a better understanding. But until we know how environment and people articulated this will not be possible.

So the book is about some not-very-long histories of people and their environment in some not-very-large areas. The approach is through loose case studies but without explicit regionality. The central purpose is to present some data and to analyse it in the context of localities. I have chosen to do this through the British Isles because they are my home.

Acknowledgements

This book owes a great debt to F.E. Zeuner who was Professor of Environmental Archaeology in the Institute of Archaeology, London University, in 1963 when I went to study under him and whose approach to archaeology was fundamentally ecological. In spite of his global chronologies, Zeuner always said that it is what was actually going on between people and their surroundings that really mattered, and that without this understanding broader interpretational schemes were useless. Of course, the book has been written in a climate where individuals and small communities are seen as increasingly important and where broad schemes of regionality, cultures and countrywide change are eschewed. So I owe much to the work of scholars over the last decade or so and especially to that of Peter Dickens and M-A Dobres. There is nothing really new in this book, and one of the things I have tried to show is how much latent information there is in published work. So I am greatly indebted, too, to the painstaking fieldwork and detailed publications that I have drawn on.

Three colleagues have been invaluable: Niall Sharples has been an encouragement and a gadfly throughout, helping with endless requests for information and references; Alasdair Whittle has shared freely his inexhaustible ideas; and Terry O'Connor, with whom I have written a completely different book, has helped magnificently with his intimate and ecological knowledge, and his wit. Douglass Bailey, Don Benson, Richard Brewer, Donald Davidson, Mary Davis, Andrew Dunwell, Charly French, Frances Griffith, Richard Hingley, Mark Lodwick, Bill Manning, Francis Pryor and Maisie Taylor helped out with photographs, references and discussions; John Morgan put up with my demands for yet more photographs and took the photograph of the Lydney dog; Howard Mason did the lettering on the line drawings; Viola Dias and Sue Virgo have always been on hand for practicalities; and Bryony Coles introduced me to the beavers of the River Bez and St Roman. I am grateful to Viscount Bledisloe for permission to photograph and publish the Lydney dog; and Andrew Dunwell for allowing me to re-draw his plan of Edin's Hall. Figures 83 and 85-88 re-drawn by permission of York Archaeological Trust.

Notes Dates are in thousands of years ago (kya), calibrated C-14 dates AD or BC, or calendrical dates from historical records; dates quoted in the form c4452/4035-4340/3985 BC refer to C-14 calibrated ranges where given in the original publications. I have used imperial measurements for land distances because these are easier to appreciate than metric ones. Other measurements in metric in the original publications are usually kept especially where precise, as with human stature. All diagrams have north at the top unless otherwise shown.

The front cover shows the Cheviot Hills from Peniel Heugh — photo by Vivian Evans.

1 Some early people

La Cotte de St Brelade (**1**) is a huge crag on the south-west coast of Jersey with several fissures running across it from one side to the other. Today the crag is grey because of chemical weathering of the rock, but in the cold periods of the Ice Age when the surface was subject to frost it was deep pink, the colour of the native granite. The crag is at the end of a sinuous ridge (**2**), and it was along this that mammoth and woolly rhinoceros were driven southwards by people to the crag. Just before the crag is reached the ground rises and then falls steeply, allowing the animals to be driven swiftly down hill out of control into the fissure and onto the ground 160ft below. For people to have killed the animals in this way it would have been necessary to guide them from their feeding grounds on the Jersey plateau and to prevent them from moving down the several valleys on either side of the narrowing ridge. People were probably posted at critical places even to the very end of the ridge overlooking Portelet Bay where there is an escape route down the slope. Vegetation may have been fired to help this, and symbiotic wolves may have aided, and even initiated, the drive. The whole process may have taken several days. In fact it may have taken a lot longer because the Jersey plateau may not have been the most natural and luxuriant feeding grounds for these animals. It has steep northern cliffs which are difficult of access and many ravines which may have been wooded and not the general habitat of the mammoth and rhino. The grasslands and tundra of the low plains around the plateau, now sea but in colder periods land (**3**), were more likely the main feeding areas of these herbivores so it was necessary to start the drive from even further away.

Bone heaps of mammoth and woolly rhinoceros have been excavated from the deposits at the foot of the fissure in La Cotte de St Brelade and, if they formed in the way just described, this implies organisation in planning and hunting. There seems no other way in which such massive bones in such quantities could have got there. Drives by wolves alone, scavenging by hyenas, carrying by humans or natural deaths on the headland or in the cave can all be discounted. Some bones are better represented than others, for example, many skulls of mammoth and rhino, more fore- than hind-limb bones of mammoth, no ankle and foot bones in one pile, and no vertebrae or ribs in another, and it is possible that these differences were caused by differential butchery, distribution and discard of particular carcass parts in particular areas. The best joints may have been distributed to important people, or to people important in the hunt such as those who first saw the herd, those who played a big part in driving it and those who were brave. Carcass use likely took place over several weeks, months or even years. Meat, brains and offal were removed fairly rapidly and intensively as a prime-niche activity; specialised extraction of ivory may have taken place over a longer period although there is no evidence for it here; later niches were

1   *La Cotte de St Brelade. The animals were driven along the skyline into the fissure which is in the middle of the photograph*

marginal with one or two people visiting the site for hide-, sinew- or marrow-processing; extended and intermittent squatter use may have involved splintering bones for fuel; while use for manufacturing tools would have been best done from bones which were completely dried and devoid of all soft matter. During periods when humans were absent, hyena scavenging may have destroyed bone parts incompletely fused, thus accounting for the absence of proximal articulations of mammoth humeri or femora in one area. The final placing of the bones before they were covered with sediment may have been through their deliberate positioning by people, and there may have been more significance to this than the mere business of tidying the floor of the fissure. Thus there is a rib which seems to have been driven through a mammoth skull, and three woolly rhinoceros skulls are placed together with several mammoth scapulae.

We do not know what may have gone on at other headlands or what may be buried in other fissures along the Jersey coast, but the feeling that La Cotte was special is strong. Thus it is not particularly close to extensive grazing lands; it is not close to suitable sources of stone for tools; and the headland is matched in grandeur and its deep pink colour by several others along the coast. Even as a game trap it involved a lot of effort, although this may have been part of the attraction. Yet the floors of the fissure and an adjacent cave have yielded many thousands of stone tools and animal bones, masses of burnt materials, and even a few human teeth. Occupation took place over thousands of years during successive warm and cold stages, perhaps from as early as 250 kya and ending around 60 kya although it was certainly not continuous. The mammoth and rhino kills, from two or possibly three occasions, were part of a strategy which involved a wider range of game like horse, red deer, giant deer, reindeer, bison or aurochs, chamois and fur-bearers like wolf, arctic fox and bear. They are only preserved because the accumulations took place just before the cave was left by people and just before influxes of wind-blown silt which buried them, occurring during cold stages when Jersey was linked to Normandy and, at times of lowest sea-level, the other Channel Islands and England. Yet these hunts, especially in their spectacle and danger, played a role in ensuring the significance of the place and in bringing together groups of people who were otherwise dispersed.

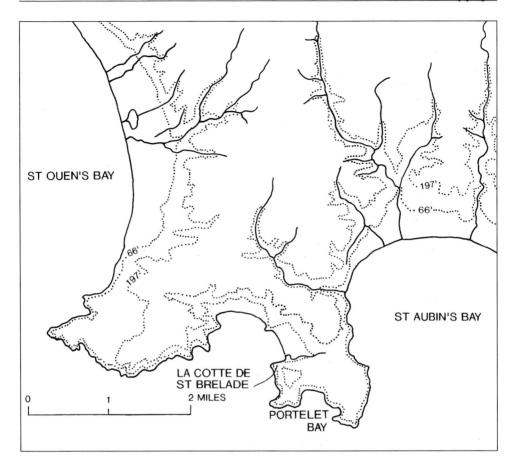

ST OUEN'S BAY

ST AUBIN'S BAY

LA COTTE DE
ST BRELADE

0   1   2 MILES

PORTELET
BAY

2　　　*South-west Jersey, the location of La Cotte de St Brelade*

Further north, two much earlier sites were in quite different environments (**4**). These are Swanscombe and Clacton in the estuary of the River Thames where flint tools and animal bones occur on the surface of low-domed gravel areas which were once part of river floodplains in warm-climate woodland. The locations were possibly where people could feel safe from dangerous animals like lions and away from competitors for carcasses like hyenas. The floodplains provided a diversity of fen and alder woodland, backswamps, gravel banks, swift currents and slack-water areas (**5**), the combined use of which allowed the stalking and killing of game. Beavers with their damming and channelling added to this diversity (**15, 16**) and wolves could have aided in the hunting drives. People may have taken parts of carcasses across river channels onto the gravel banks or they may have scavenged dead animals already there.

At Clacton-on-Sea the site was almost at sea-level although there was no brackish influence. The flint artefacts were associated with bones of giant deer, red deer, fallow deer, horse, giant beaver, two species of rhinoceros (neither of them woolly), straight-tusked and another species of elephant, aurochs, bison and wild boar. Pollen

3   *View from La Cotte. In the Ice Age this was dry land*

suggests an environment of mixed-oak woodland at around 400 kya. Associated peat beds yielded a pointed yew stick usually referred to as the Clacton spearpoint because it is thought to have been artificially pointed and used in hunting. Experimental manufacture of a similar yew stick with contemporary stone tools suggests that the 'Clactonian notch' — a flint flake with a concave retouch — was the most suitable tool for the purpose. The stick is about 37cm long and with a maximum diameter of 3.6cm, so it is quite robust and could have been the end of a thrusting spear used in close-quarter hunting. The break may have occurred in action, perhaps as it was used in the manner of a *Saufeder* in hunting boar, with one person standing with it embedded in the soil while others drove the boar towards him and onto it. This dangerous sport may have been highly prestigious and the selection of yew wood for the spear may have been for its associations with poison, the redness of the wood, and the peculiar property of the trees of 'bleeding' as much as for its hardness and flexibility.

At Swanscombe in Kent (**4**), abundant flint artefacts and animal bones lay in sands and fine gravels in a shallow channel. The surface of this, the Lower Gravel, at c82 to 85ft OD (25.1 to 25.9m) is probably the same sort of age, c420 kya, as the Clacton-on-Sea surface, the difference in height probably being due to downwarping at Clacton. Above this in the Lower Loam, deposited in quiet-water conditions, there were numerous animal footprints some with skid-marks and splashes around them which formed when deposition had ceased temporarily and the surface partially dried out; some areas were even marked with raindrops. There was some sequence to these, with the large mammal footprints being less distinct and made in shallow water and the small mammal footprints overlying them being more distinct and made in partially dried mud. The bovid (cattle or bison) footprints show more traces of skidding than the cervid (deer) ones so it seems that herds of the two species passed over the area on separate occasions when conditions were different. There were flint knapping areas with the flints just where they had been left by the knappers, and many pieces could be refitted. One area was adjacent to the skull and antlers of a fallow deer and it is suggested that the carcass may have attracted the knappers to this spot. The raw material was local gravel flint. Some of the nodules had been brought in already partially worked and then, after flaking, the cores had been removed — as had the bones of the fallow deer. So even at this remote time we can see some of the individual activities of people, animals and weather on this river bed.

As well as the large mammals at Swanscombe which were of similar species to those

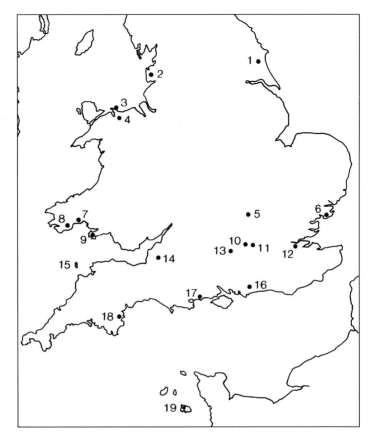

4   Sites mentioned in
       chaps 1 & 2.

1, Gransmoor;
2, Poulton-le-Fylde;
3, Kendrick's Cave;
4, Pontnewydd;
5, Pitstone;
6, Clacton;
7, Coygan Cave;
8, Hoyle's Mouth;
9, Paviland;
10, Furze Platt;
11, Baker's Farm;
12, Swanscombe;
13, Thatcham;
14, Gough's Cave;
15, Lundy;
16, Boxgrove;
17, Hengistbury Head;
18, Kent's Cavern;
19, La Cotte de St
Brelade

from Clacton, including three species of rhinoceros, there were birds — golden eye, cormorant, wood pigeon and osprey — and salmon which may have been part of the human diet. Molluscs and pollen indicate local alder woodland with areas of dry ground and, late on, some woodland recession which may have been caused by concentrations of animals and human activity at the river edge. At other sites of the same sort of age in southern England, woodland reduction is associated with fire. Although the inference that any of this is related to human activity is circumstantial, it is attractive to think of hunting as having taken place in areas where animals came to the river to wallow and drink, with people driving them into the river and generally confusing them, especially in areas of burning undergrowth or fen, until they could be speared or drowned and washed up on gravel banks.

Still at Swanscombe, above the Lower Loam there are the Middle Gravels which yielded fragments of a human skull, probably of a young woman. The species was *Homo heidelbergensis* or an early form of *Homo sapiens neanderthalensis*. A type of stone artefact called a handaxe occurs prolifically in these Middle Gravels. These are of various shapes, sometimes pointed at one end, sometimes rounded. They combine strength with sharpness and ease of use because they fit into the hand, and are much more efficient in cutting, scraping and butchering than simple flakes which are more difficult to hold, break more easily and are less easy to re-sharpen. Specific shape differences may be due

5   *The River Bez in southern France*

to stylistic preferences of different groups of hominids and the close similarity in form and detail of handaxes from two sites in the Thames Valley less than 5 miles apart, Furze Platt, near Maidenhead, and Baker's Farm, near Slough, suggests that copying took place. The most symmetrical specimens are beautiful and this was the main reason for their early collection by antiquarians; but many are not symmetrical at all and really quite crude. Wear analysis has failed to show a consistent use or consistency of use although several functions like cutting meat have been demonstrated. Many people in these early times in a variety of types of site seem to have got on very well without them, as at Clacton-on-Sea, in the Lower Gravel and Lower Loam at Swanscombe, and for most of the time at La Cotte de St Brelade. One suggestion is that they were used to butcher carcasses when there was competition from carnivores or when speed was otherwise crucial as in the need to feed young. More likely is that they were made when there was some kind of pressure generally, not just competition from carnivores, but in rivalry between human groups where territories overlapped, when there was a scarcity of carcasses, or when there was a need to demonstrate superiority as when males were trying to attract mates. They were an expression of a need, a communication. Once this passed — and it seldom lasted long — they were abandoned, often in huge numbers.

Handaxes were prolific at the site of Boxgrove in Sussex (**4**). This was a coastal site when it was occupied by early humans, but now it is over 7 miles from the sea and 141ft above sea-level. It was occupied by *Homo heidelbergensis*, whose teeth and a leg bone have been found in the deposits. This site was even earlier than Clacton and Swanscombe, dating to c500 kya. Sea-level was falling and the coastal chalk cliff near where people were living was crumbling. Massive flint nodules were being exposed and these were sometimes collected and carried to the locations of animal carcasses where they were used for handaxe manufacture which in turn were used for butchery. Sometimes just the finished handaxes were brought to the carcasses. The occupation was in scrub and grassland, perhaps kept open by grazing animals. There were surface undulations with wetter and drier areas, and it was on the drier areas that butchery took place. Bones of red deer and bison show traces of human modification in the form of linear striations and impact damage where filleting and marrow extraction occurred, and there were individual animal butchery locations of a horse and a rhinoceros. A horse shoulder blade had a third of an almost circular hole 4cm diameter which may have been made with a wooden spear, the fracturing and rifling of the bone-break suggesting puncturing at high speed as from a javelin. And even if the Clacton stick is not a spear and the Boxgrove horse scapula hole not caused by one, spears were certainly in use at around this time as seen in several recently discovered at Schöningen, near Helmstedt, in Germany.

Boxgrove was at a gap in the high chalk sea-cliff which was an extremely prominent backdrop to the site; today it is a low slope. A river ran through the gap, there were ponds on the land surface and, in places, intertidal lagoons. The gap was a communication route between the coastal plain and the dry chalk plateau where there was woodland, and it is likely that animals and hominids moved back and forth between these areas to exploit the different environments. The Boxgrove site may indeed have been located to take advantage of the concentration and predictable occurrence of game in the area, perhaps with different human groups overlapping there. The abundance of handaxes and their fine quality may be explained in competition between such groups for carcasses, and perhaps also with animal scavengers who were similarly attracted to the area. It is true that there may have been mutual avoidance as occurs between the Masai and lions in Kenya today, as I have been told by Anna Perry who lives there, but this cannot have been absolute, and the threat of animal carnivores may have allowed competitive display of superiority in handaxe manufacture, especially if members of the opposite sex were watching. Some of the handaxes are extremely thin, symmetrical and flaked almost with parallel precision. They are also razor-sharp. A few have oblique tranchet flakes removed across the tip as a late episode in their manufacture, and the flakes from these occur among the butchery debris; in some cases there has even been retouch of the handaxes across the tranchet scars. So the handaxes and the carcasses provided a focus for interactions and these were enhanced through the larger locale of the animal carnivores and the gap. It was all quite complex.

Boxgrove is one of the earliest known sites in the British Isles and it is reasonable to suppose that there are others of earlier date yet to be discovered. People may have been present here from at least 700 kya as they were in Europe. There were new niches to be established, unfamiliar from those in southern Europe, south-west Asia and north Africa from where our people had come. How did they do this? The broad river valleys of northern France and southern England as well as the now-submerged lands of the English Channel, the Severn Estuary and the southern part of the North Sea may have provided grazing lands for game animals whose dead carcasses at least, if not their living bodies, were a rich source of food. But now tolerance of cold and oceanicity was needed. The Boxgrove leg bone indicates a robust adult nearly 6ft tall and thus without the adaptations of stockiness to cold climate which were to come later with the Neanderthalers. Winters were especially problematic in the snow-covered lands. The Clacton pointed stick may have been a spear but it may also have been used as a snow-probe to locate animal carcasses beneath the snow; fire could have been used to control their thawing so not all the meat was melted at once.

Altogether, there were plenty of interactions between people and animals such as group drives and associations with wolves, the quarrying and working of inorganic materials, the use of fire and the monumentality of specific land features. There may not have been much awareness of long distances but interactions were still complex and intimate. People and other predators knew where their prey animals were living and breeding, what sort of state they were in and how they moved around. Wolves and humans may have created bone debris that was either wolf-specific or people-specific, often in different areas of a single site **(p. 20)**, but these were in a wider sphere of interactions between wolves and people generally. Rivalries between humans and wolves in hunting and just in moving around were probably expressed by using particular areas, or by hunting particular herds of cattle or individuals, while the distributions of the cattle related not only to what the humans and wolves were doing but to rivalries in spacing and mating behaviour between bulls and their cows. The hunt went on all the time in people's minds and in their behaviour and was being continually modified in relation to various influences of the practical and expressive orders.

Carcasses, too, were important, as media through which people could increase their status and reproductive fitness, as Bernd Heinrich has described for ravens in his book, *Ravens in winter*. One person alone might take a practical and rapid approach or even ignore the carcass; two or more people of the same sex might draw out the business in an expression of rivalries; two or more people of the same sex with another of the opposite sex watching might also introduce an element of display. This also took place through the medium of handaxes, which, although not unknown from southern Europe, are especially prolific at certain times in northern France and southern England and may have symbolised the establishment of new niches there. The cool manufacture of handaxes by young *Homo heidelbergensis* males against a backdrop of lions would have been a strong attraction for onlooking females.

Gottfried von Strasburg's *Tristan* shows the importance of butchery in expressing relationships between people of different customs and between people and their dogs. Through the butchery of a deer information about each other was gleaned and friendships were made.

> 'How now, master, what is that meant to be?' interposed Tristan, bred as he was in courtly ways . . . 'Whoever saw a hart broken up in this fashion? . . . The usage is different in the land where I was reared' . . . Tristan, the boy so far from home, removed his cloak, placed it on a tree-stump, tucked up his robe, and rolled up his sleeves. Then he smoothed down his hair and laid it above his ears . . .

And after the butchery, involving many technical terms and in which different people are called on to help in different parts of the process:

> He chopped the milt and the lungs, and then the paunch and the great gut into suitably small pieces and spread it all out on the hide. This done, he summoned the hounds . . . They were all there in a trice, standing over their reward. 'There you are', said the eloquent youth, 'this is what they call the quarry at home . . . And believe me it was devised for the good of the hounds. It is a beneficial practice since the bits one lays on the hide serve to flesh the hounds'. 'Lord!' they all said, 'what do you mean dear child? We clearly see that these arts were devised to the great good of bloodhounds and the pack!'

Tristan even explains the cutting of withies, the trussing of the butchered portions and the conveying of the head to King Mark's court **(p. 148)**. 'The huntsman and his men were once again amazed that the boy should propound so many hunting usages one after the another and with such discernment, and be so well versed in such lore'. This was how localities were established and how they worked.

In this chapter I have introduced some ideas about how people may have communicated through topographical intersections like Boxgrove, rock formations like La Cotte de St Brelade, activities like hunting and butchery, and stone tools like handaxes. I have shown how there are different depths and kinds of meaning in all of these and how they could have mediated in interactions among people. And I have suggested that these interactions could have had behavioural consequences which went beyond the mere practicalities of survival, as in expressions of display.

2 To the end of the Ice Age

On either side of him the thunderous Sunday orchestras of Europe rolled out their massive melodies: but he . . . unbelievably ancient, went on with his unillusioned chant . . . He knew, where we believed.

TH White, *The goshawk*

From the time of the Last Warm Stage at c120 kya until the end of the Ice Age at c8000 BC it is difficult to resist seeing human activities as being a response to environment. There were several secular and massive changes of climate, there were variations in the degree to which the British Isles were cut off from the continent by the seas, and there is our peripheral position generally in relation to Europe. However, the situation is complicated because there were global changes taking place at this time in the distribution, physical characteristics, material culture and behaviour of people, and it is difficult to disentangle these from changes which may have been specific to the British Isles. Furthermore, we should not equate levels of diversity and abundance of material culture with those of population density or vitality. It is especially important that absence of evidence should not be assumed to mean absence of people and conveniently correlated with difficult living conditions. There were plenty of locales for communication that did not need or leave a pretentious signal in material culture. So the more visible archaeology after these so-called blank periods may need to be assessed in terms of indigenous people rather than recolonisation.

Thus the difficulties of living in extensive deciduous woodland and of getting to the islands in the first place due to their isolation from the Continent by very high sea-levels are often seen as the reasons for the absence of people during the Last Warm Stage. However, people at this time were colonising the East Indies and Australasia and this involved the use of boats and several sea voyages, so there seems no intrinsic reason why the British Isles with only a single crossing could not have been colonised similarly. Of course, planned sea-colonisation required not just technology but motivation as well as cognition about a likely outcome. Then, equally, it may not have been planned at all but have been the incidental result of certain sectors of the population trying to impress others with their sea-going skills. And even if people did reach these islands in the Last Warm Stage, living in the woodlands may have been easier than we think. Thus we should forget about the global picture of an apparently low level of human evolutionary development at this time and the apparently late colonisation of woodland, both of which may be wrong. Further, there seems no intrinsic reason why people should not have been as able to live on animals that were small, secretive, and went around in small groups as they were on the large and visible herds of grasslands. And as for the absence of artefacts, there were sound practical reasons for this such as the absence of intense social interactions in communities of small group size and the weakness of competition at the kill.

People were definitely present in the British Isles from c60 kya. Deciduous woodland gave way to tundra and grassland, with periods of coniferous and birch woodland. The main characteristics of the human niche until c35 kya were low density, wide dispersal of sites, discontinuous and short occupations, and a similar distribution to that of previous groups, namely southern Britain. Hunting of mammoth and other large animals like woolly rhino and horse continued to be a mainstay of survival. There were interactions with spotted hyenas. Coygan Cave (**4**) in South Wales on a headland above a coastal marsh was occupied somewhere between 64 and 38 kya and could have been used in a similar manner to La Cotte de St Brelade. The distribution of a distinctive kind of handaxe with angled junctions between sides and the broader end is partially along river valleys, suggesting their use — handaxes and valleys — in communication. Anticipatory behaviour and planning is shown in the mixture of local and foreign stone used for artefacts at several sites, at Coygan from over 60 miles away. In Europe, several *Bos* and *Bison* sites show the selective hunting of prime animals by the use of specific topography and with the same sites being used over long periods.

People at this time were Neanderthalers, *Homo sapiens neanderthalensis*, and had been so in Europe from at least 200 kya. In the British Isles the earliest known occupation was at Pontnewydd Cave in North Wales (**4**). The hominid teeth from La Cotte de St Brelade are also Neanderthal, with thick prismatic roots and large pulp cavities (the latter condition known as taurodontism). The main period of extreme Neanderthals in Europe was after the Last Warm Stage and especially from between c55 and 35 kya, and their physique is an adaptation to the cold climate. They were especially squat, short-limbed and robust, with strong bones and muscularity, and considerable signs of tooth use perhaps in lieu of tools. The peripherality of the British Isles may have led to extreme anatomical and behavioural features through genetic bottle-necking and founder effects, and spread into Europe from our islands may have enhanced the extreme nature of the Neanderthals there. Alternatively, our people may have been a more modern form of *Homo sapiens*, descended from Boxgrove through Swanscombe, and ultimately to *H. sapiens sapiens* as at Kent's Cavern (31 kya) and the burial at Paviland (26 kya). Neanderthals and *H. sapiens sapiens* were generally contemporaneous in south-west Asia and south-west Europe, in the former perhaps from as early as 90 kya, for the latter between c37-30 kya, and they may have been so in Britain. Unfortunately all this is speculation because apart from the two early sites of La Cotte de St Brelade and Pontnewydd, there are no finds of Neanderthals from the British Isles.

From c37 kya and until the glacial maximum at c18 kya, several new features occur — the appearance of *Homo sapiens sapiens*, the use of distinctive artefact types over relatively narrow time periods, the use of ivory, the use of sea-shells as decoration, and human burial. There is a similarity between these and earlier occupations in their overall southern British distribution (**4**), the low density of sites, the low density of artefacts and bone at many of the sites, and the absence of long continuous use. The new features are about

6   *Paviland from the sea*

communication and may relate to cooling climate, lowering resource productivity, and the need to maintain co-operative relations between widely dispersed groups; human-female figurines, c26 kya, performed the same function in Europe. But they may also be related to hierarchisation which needed a clear extra-somatic means of expression; or they may, as purely technological innovations, have led to such structuring in the first place. Importantly, these changes do not imply greater community complexity or humanisation. The use of a diversity of specific stone tools is just another way of communicating which happens to have left a more durable trace than the means which were at hand during earlier periods.

The Paviland Caves are in a glorious setting in a high limestone cliff in the south coast of the South Wales Gower Peninsula (**6, 7**). They are old sea-caves, carved out during the high seas of earlier warm stages and now reasonably dry. Access from the Gower plateau is down a steep dry valley called Foxhole Slade. The caves are in a great buttress of rock, invisible as approached from the plateau and down the slade until you come around to face them from the south. Access was also from the land to the south, where there is now the Bristol Channel, which stretched as a plain across to the Devon coast and many miles to the west. It was interrupted by deep gorges so crossing it would not have been easy.

In some ways the situation was very similar to Boxgrove. Animals and people could get to a variety of environments — the grasslands of the coastal plain, the hinterlands of the Gower plateau, and acidic grasslands to the north and west — and probably moved from plateau to plain through Foxhole Slade. Crossing this ecological divide in either direction was likely to have been significant, especially if different groups of people were involved. Negotiation may have been needed, if not between one group and another, then certainly in people's minds, and this could have been done through the caves, especially where they were used for burial. Thus around 26 kya the cave immediately next to the gap on the west side was complemented by the burial of a young male *Homo sapiens sapiens*, placed in the bottom of a large pothole near the entrance. It was accompanied by perforated seashells and the bones of large animals including mammoth. It was covered in red ochre, of a similar colour to the granite of La Cotte de St Brelade. In addition to the main entrance, the cave is linked to the outside by a chimney high up on the wall and this has a flat area inside it which could have been used as a shrine. When you look out from the cave (**8**) you can see Lundy Island exactly opposite on the horizon, and at the time of the burial this

7   *Paviland, detail; the cave with the burial is the large oblique opening to the left of the valley, at the level of the Last Warm Stage shore platform*

would have appeared as a massive rock plateau rising straight up out of the plain. Along the cliff at the same height are three smaller caves (**6**) which, too, may have been used as shrines and for burials. Below these fossil caves are several others which are still being eroded by the sea (**7**) but which could have been used for habitation at the time of the burial. Some of them have freshwater streams running out of them so they would have been favoured for this as well as their shelter.

After Paviland and until c13 kya there is practically no record of people in the British Isles, a feature usually attributed to the intense cold. This was the period which saw the fullest extent of ice-sheets and glaciers. It was a still and largely mineral world. Yet the ice did not actually affect most of the areas which had seen previous human occupation and there were animals, including wolf, lion, spotted hyena (at Coygan Cave until c24 kya), woolly rhinoceros, mammoth and, at Little Hoyle, Pembrokeshire, (18.45+/-0.43 kya) brown bear, red fox, hare, reindeer and collared lemming. So there were food chains and animal companions, and people were so tough and adventurous that it is likely that they were present too. Population density was probably low in the conditions of low productivity, and the people may have lived in small groups; infants may have been killed and old people sent away or left to die, as Velma Wallis wonderfully describes in her classic book, *Two old women*. But still groups could have met and exchanged ideas and marriage partners. There were people at Paviland until at least 21 kya, while in Europe the period saw the first occurrences of spearthrowers (at 18 kya) and boomerangs (20 kya) at this time. 'Bleak' rather than 'blank' may describe this period better.

The closing millennia of the Last Cold Stage (14-10 kya) saw rapid environmental changes and it is again hard not to see correlations with human activities. By 13 kya the climate was becoming as warm as it is today although more continental, ecosystem productivity was increasing, grassland and juniper and willow scrub were giving way to birch woodland, and there was a rich mammal and bird fauna. Herbivorous mammals included giant deer, elk, red deer, horse, bison, aurochs and mammoth, with a short episode of saiga antelope; carnivores included brown bear, red fox and wolf. The rapidly wasting ice-sheets and valley glaciers were leaving ponds and lakes everywhere.

Rupert Housley and his colleagues, seeing Britain during the previous millennia of the glacial maximum as being totally depopulated, suggest a two-phase re-colonisation. First there was a 'pioneer phase' c13 kya when small groups moved into the British Isles from the Continent, hunting single species like horse seasonally. This was followed by a 'residential-camp phase' of larger occupations, and with the exploitation of a more diverse fauna, including red deer and cattle, allowing more flexibility. The herds were hunted in relation to topographical features like the Cheddar Gorge or Hengistbury Head. However, this model presupposes that recolonisation overrides more individual-group behaviours and tactics, and is only relevant, too, if people were absent during the previous cold millennia.

From c13 kya, people were widely and abundantly present, living in caves and open areas, hunting the animals with spears and traps and living side by side with carnivores (**4**). They were present on the south coast of England at Hengistbury Head in Hampshire 12.5 kya where they were deliberately breaking flint blades and flakes to make tools; they aborted an elk hunt at Poulton le Fylde in Lancashire 12.4 kya when the animal which they had wounded with barbed bone points went into a lake; they were butchering and eating horse and red deer and using their tendons at Gough's Cave in Cheddar Gorge in the Mendip Hills 12.8-12.1 kya where the remains of the bones were taken into the back of the cave by wolves and foxes; at the same site they were dismembering human corpses and they may have cut the tongue out of a human jaw; they may have precipitated the extinction of mammoth from the British Isles by 12.0 kya; at Gransmoor in the lake district of south-east Yorkshire, they left an antler barbed point (with pine-pitch hafting residue) in lake muds embedded in a log 11.5-11.1 kya, and they left several others in the same area; and at Pitstone, Buckinghamshire, towards the end of the period, they may have been firing vegetation.

After 12 kya conditions were unsettled, and 11.5-11.0 kya was very cold. Renewed corrie glaciation took place in the mountains, soil instability led to inwashing of material into lakes, and woodland, rich fen and reedswamp were destroyed. The diversity of the mammal fauna fell, giant deer became extinct, but reindeer reappeared for the first time since the glacial maximum. People used new types of distinctive tanged points as spearheads, and the bow-and-arrow was probably used c10.1 kya for the first time. There may have been large settlements in autumn and winter associated with high densities of reindeer, perhaps on migration routes. Bone and antler were used for artefacts and people may have stored the antler in caches in lakes to prevent it from decaying and being scavenged by animals. Sites of medium size were occupied in spring and summer, these in the valleys close to reindeer migration routes as well as in uplands where horse and red deer were hunted. Small sites were only occupied in summer and were exclusively upland.

*8   View from within the
      Paviland Cave*

This model, in which the intensive use of reindeer was seasonal, not year round, and exploitation was only possible with the integrated use of horse and red deer, is based on work in the Rhine-Donau area but could also apply to Britain. There is a horse mandible decorated with incised chevrons from Kendrick's Cave in North Wales, 10 kya. But it is difficult to generalise because of variations in reindeer spacing behaviour, dispersal vs. aggregation, for example, depending on population density as much as season.

Temperature rise from arctic to present levels took place c10 kya and may have been achieved in 50-100 years, although there were still short reversals. Juniper scrub and steppe of Chenopodiaceae, mugwort (*Artemisia*) and crowberry (*Empetrum*) (**9**) gave way to birch woodland. The fauna once again was diverse and now it included pig, roe deer and badger which had been absent previously. The reindeer was absent; the horse and elk persisted for a few centuries, to c9.3 kya, occurring in the Kennet Valley at Thatcham; wolves, foxes and bears were the main carnivores.

We should be careful about equating human innovations at this time with changes in the biophysical environment, especially when they did not take place a few millennia earlier in the context of similar ecological changes. The bow-and-arrow, for example, may not have been used as the most efficient way of exploiting the fauna of the closing woodland but more as a need for expression in a new technology and in the diversity of arrowhead types (or microliths) this entailed. Axes and dug-out boats, being used now

9   Artemisia *and Chenopodiaceae steppe*

for the first time, may have been more about the establishment of localities through prestige artefacts and activities rather than a need for water transport and its satisfaction in the availability of trees. The increasing range of animals eaten, especially a dependence on wild fowl, need not have been just a reflection of the greater diversity afforded by the woodlands. It may be related to the greater difficulties of getting enough fat from mammals, which now had fewer problems surviving the winter, as well as to the needs in this of pregnant women, especially if women were now taking on new roles. The different animals being hunted may have been an expression of territoriality as people spread into previously unoccupied habitats and areas of the British Isles — uplands, northern England, Scotland, the islands and Ireland — rather than a direct response to what was available. New localities and niches like uplands and islands were expressions of identity as much as relations of ecology.

In this chapter I have suggested that prominence of material culture is not about the need for increased communication in the context of changing environments, and that there were activities of a more ephemeral kind through which localities could have been established. Accordingly I have played down the idea that people responded to the biophysical environment, especially its climate and vegetation. The apparent correlations between human population densities and climate change in the last 120,000 years perhaps need re-evaluation.

3 Fforest Fawr, Dartmoor and the East Anglian fen-edge

Lakes and bogs

The importance of water goes right back — for the water itself and for its ecotonal properties, the giving of diversity and change to the land. Lakes were a focus for repeated use by animals and people, not just as hunting traps or for their economic value or security, but also for their serenity. They may also have been sacred, and the Poulton-le-Fylde elk may have been as much a sacrifice as a failed hunt. The destruction of sedge fen, reeds and bulrush (*Scirpus lacustris*) swamp around lakes by slopewash from the surrounding land during the eleventh and twelfth millennia **(p. 20)** was probably a far more significant event in people's lives than the climatic cooling which engendered it. Intensive animal use had the same effect as can be seen today where cattle destroy the zonation around lakes and bring the grassland to the water's edge **(62)**, while the introduction of phosphate, dung and organic matter can destroy much of the life in the lakes themselves.

Human communities settled around lakes and left their tools, their woodworking endeavours, animal bones and blackened layers of burnt reeds and trees. Eventually vegetation built up and covered these remains with peat. In deeper waters, fine organic muds accumulated and raised the bottom which eventually merged with the edge deposits. There was often an extensive reedswamp phase when the whole of a basin was covered with reeds, succeeded by woodland of birch, willow or alder, known as 'carr.' There was much variation, but ultimately the hydrology entailed the formation of vegetation which tolerated acidic and wet conditions, made up mainly of species of *Sphagnum* moss, cotton grass (actually a sedge) (*Eriophorum* spp.), and shrubs like crowberry (*Empetrum nigrum*) and heather (*Calluna vulgaris*). This is raised bog, known as such because it is often domed and can be several feet or even tens of feet thick. There were periods when it dried out and when woodland grew over the bog leaving layers of tree stumps in it; and there were times when it was flooded, especially around the edges — the lagg — when plants which prefer calcareous waters like the saw-toothed sedge (*Cladium mariscus*) and water snails like *Lymnaea peregra* thrived. But the ultimate environment, unless drained by humans for farmland, which is the fate of most of these basins today, was raised bog.

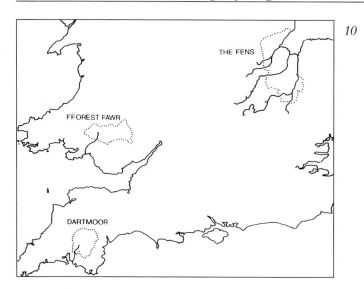

10 The areas discussed in chap. 3

How it works

We could think about the interactions of people and environment in terms of different land-forms like upland and coast and at a scale of several hundreds of square miles. However, this implies that these were relevant in human lives, which may not have been the case: if we look at things regionally, regional patterns emerge. This sort of scale of enquiry, too, is likely to start us thinking about various kinds of land-use strategies, and especially mobilities, which equally may never have existed. Mobility is easy to suggest because it is fashionable and because most biological data reflect exploitation at particular seasons. But until we have unequivocal evidence, like refitting of artefacts between sites or stable isotope analysis of human bones for different locations of diet, mobility of a specific group of people on a seasonal basis in a regional system should not be assumed. So I am going to look at small areas and the human interactions in these (**10**).

Waun Fignen Felen

From around 10,000 BC, numerous lakes allowed the use of high uplands by cattle, deer, people and wolves when they might otherwise have been deserted. This was so in the Carmarthenshire Fans of South Wales at a place called Waun Fignen Felen where there was settlement by groups of hunters around a closing lake at c1600ft above sea-level (**11**). People were in contact over some distance as shown by the raw materials of the artefacts — beach flint (18 miles) and Greensand chert (50 miles), mainly for arrowheads and butchery knives, and mudstone (62 miles) for beads. The artefacts were on an old soil surface, or beneath its humus layer, buried beneath peat. The earliest occupation, c7300 BC, is represented by a broad-blade technology and took place in the lake-edge reed swamp during a general expansion of hazel woodland. It was probably a summer occupation from which red deer and cattle were hunted as suggested by the high altitude of the location and the low-diversity artefact assemblages; the lack of lithic scavenging

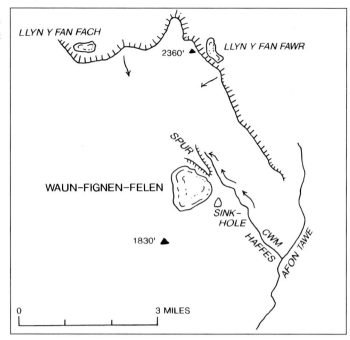

11   Waun-Fignen-Felen, with the directions in which hunters may have approached the lake (arrows). (Based on Smith & Cloutman 1988)

and the discrete nature of the assemblages also suggest specialised, short-stay, activities. A later occupation occurred c6500 BC with a narrow-blade technology. This included microliths, probably from multiple-component arrowheads, and perhaps even from individual hunting losses in the lake itself since they were found in two tight groups, one of twelve nearly identical microliths and one of fourteen fragments which refitted to give a minimum of six microliths.

Raised bog began to form c8000 BC after clearance of woodland, and may have been a response to this as well as to burning; or the woodland may have been killed by the build up of the peat. Fire may have been used by humans to clear the woodland although Nick Barton and his team, who have done the most recent work in the area, find this unconvincing in view of the light woodland generally and the presence of people in the area long before peat growth started. More likely is the burning of *Empetrum*-heathland between c5400-5100 BC which would have promoted the growth of fresh shoots and thus encouraged deer.

At different scales and for different reasons Waun Fignen Felin was attractive and it was visited repeatedly over several millennia. It was, and still is, a distinctive and closely defined feature ringed around by low hills (**11**). Even after the infilling of the lake, the area was still prominent as, first, a reedswamp, then woodland of successively birch, hazel and alder, then a raised bog, treeless in more wooded land, and today a black eroding bog; and there was always water available as streams or laggs. There is an adjacent deep sinkhole with strangely polished black limestone rocks in its base which may have had a ritual meaning. Some of the hills around have small limestone crags on them which may have attracted animals and been the nuclei of clearings from which the lake could have been observed. The approach from the south is up the Haffes River which is a deep gorge for most of its course with a spectacular waterfall part way up. The lie of the land meant that people could have approached the lake or bog ultimately from the east, against the prevailing wind and hidden by a low ridge until the very end (**11**). From the north, the approach involved climbing from the base of the Fans escarpment, past two corrie lakes, and up a steep chimney onto the plateau. From there on down to Waun Fignen Felen there was little cover, unless it was lightly wooded, but a strategy involving some hunters waiting at the lake in the reedswamp or on the limestone crags above it and others driving game towards it from the grazing lands in the north is realistic. Like the game drives of earlier periods, wolves might have assisted in this. But now things were different because by this stage the wolves which were associated with humans may have been tame and on the way to domestication. And if the ones from Star Carr in north-east Yorkshire are anything to go by they may have accompanied people from their winter quarters on the coast up into the hills. As a site of symbolism in access Waun Fignen Felen was magnificent. In the eighth millennium BC the area was a part of the highest and most extensive upland grazings in the whole of the Carmarthenshire Fans and this, together with the several lakes in the area, may have been the main reason for its attractiveness for animals and humans. It was a singular place. They could see across from the hills around the bog southwards to the peatlands and clays of Swansea Bay, which, too, may have provided habitats for hunters and their wolves in the winter. To the west is Mynydd Preseli and to the north the hills of mid-Wales.

Dartmoor

Another area where there was hunting in the uplands in the earlier part of the Holocene is Dartmoor (**12**). There are no lakes, mainly because the area was free of ice in the Last Ice Age, but there are plenty of hollows and valleys, and in some of these peat has accumulated. The plateau is covered in blanket peat above c1575ft, although this extends down to some poorly-drained areas as low as 1475ft, while the lower slopes below c1300ft are enclosed fields and settlements. Between these two zones there is mainly open moorland of grass on mineral soils, although there are a few areas of woodland (**13**).

Before the development of blanket peat, the woodland was more extensive although it never covered all of the plateau. In the north at Black Ridge Brook at 1870ft OD there was heathland and trees c5700 BC which had given way to open heath, scattered hazel and some pockets of blanket peat by 4300 BC; lower down at Pinswell, 1512ft, there was hazel woodland. Around Blacklane Brook in the south, there was oak and hazel woodland, with much heather and grasses although these may be from the local bog vegetation. There were always some open areas on Dartmoor, and tree remains from beneath the blanket peat above 1300ft are few. Even at the maximum woodland extent at Blacka Brook in the south as low as 885ft there were unwooded areas. Presumably the uplands were kept open by grazing animals, wind and the inherently poor granite soils because there are no general climatic reasons why woodland should not once have covered the entire moor.

But there was structure to these open areas provided by the inter-relationships of animals and the land. Deer and cattle probably concentrated around the tor bases because they provided shelter, back-scratching areas, and territorial markers as they do for the

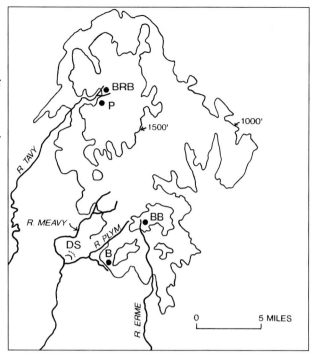

12   Dartmoor.
B, Blacka Brook;
BB, Blacklane Brook;
BRB, Black Ridge Brook;
DS, Dewerstone;
P, Pinswell.
(Based on Simmons et al.
1983)

sheep and cattle today. The concentration of grazing, trampling and manuring probably created a halo of open vegetation around the tors which themselves were likely wooded where tree seedlings were protected in the cracks of the rock. Individual trees were also a focus for animals, with the same sort of effects (**14**). Water accumulated in small hollows created by animals around stones (**67**) and at the bases of trees where roots grew over each other. There was also likely encroachment at the woodland edge where animals sheltered, where they browsed on the more diverse vegetation, and where they could see predators for long distances. In the valleys, river edges were also important, both for water and as tracks. Open areas along water courses were created by beavers who felled trees, dammed the rivers and caused flooding which in turn killed more trees (**15, 16, 17**). At first it was the beaver pools which attracted the cattle and deer; then, when abandonment of the dams led to their collapse, it was the rich herbaceous vegetation in the drained areas which was important to them. Lynx and wolves, perhaps using the tors as dens, went between the tors, the woodland edges and the water courses, preying on young beaver, deer and cattle. People understood these behaviours and came to see the tors, the large trees and the rivers for their concentrations of animals, their high diversity of fruits and nuts, and perhaps for their sacredness as well. Thus it was that there was considerable organisation in the land even before any deliberate clearances by people or the formation of blanket peat.

At Black Ridge Brook, a valley site at 1466ft, and Pinswell about 200yds away further up the slope at 1512ft, peat formed locally before c6785 BC in dense birch woodland. Then, from 5700 to 4300 BC, charcoal indicates burning, and there was an increase of heather (*Calluna*) and the ocurrence of the fire-resistant cow-wheat, aptly named *Melampyrum*. Woodland, now hazel-dominated, with some oak and alder, drew back. Acid grassland

27

13   Wistman's Wood, Dartmoor

with sorrels (*Rumex* spp.) persisted for several centuries before blanket peat began to form around 4000 BC. As studied by Peter Moore, these changes may have been caused by waterlogging consequent on woodland removal, the formation of an impermeable iron pan and the clogging of soil pores by charcoal from the fires; lowering of soil pH and a reduction of microbial activity through the growth of *Sphagnum* moss were probably contributory factors. The blanket peat extended from suitable foci on shelves and in depressions in lower areas, while at the same time expanding generally from the open summits and higher slopes. There was much small-scale land diversity, with areas of grassland and heath, areas where blanket peat was forming, and others where trees were growing up again, all adding to the diversity already created by the animals.

In the fourth and third millennia BC, when farming communities were becoming established, there was some woodland clearance. An enclosure called the Dewerstone may belong to this time. It is on the south edge of the moor on a promontory at the end of a long interfluve between the Rivers Plym and Meavy at 700ft OD (**18**). The valleys are practically gorges here, and the earthworks of the enclosure and a line of stones are only present on the north side of the promontory, thus effectively cutting it off. The most impressive view is from the north-east from where the site is seen as an island of open grassland cleared of boulders and surrounded on its steep sides by woodland. It is all very evocative of the causewayed camps of this time **(p. 68)**, although there is no certainty that the Dewerstone is fourth millennium. The location is also ideally suited as the end of a game drive. It has the same combination of features that we saw at La Cotte — a long

14   *A holly tree on Dartmoor showing the differential development of grazed grassland underneath it in contrast to the tussocky grass elsewhere*

sinuous ridge, a steep slope down, a short slope up to a tor and then the cliff — and we can also note the Dolmen de Couperon on Jersey in the same sort of context **(p. 79)**. The location may have been chosen too for its more general siting at a major joining of two rivers and at the boundary between farmland and the wilder more open land of the moor. There is a good view to the coast at Plymouth.

On the other side of the Plym gorge from the Dewerstone is Shaugh Moor, rising to c900ft (**18, 21**). This is an area of upland settlement and enclosure dating from c1500 to 2000 BC. A boundary bank, the Saddlesborough reeve, crosses the moor on the watershed, separating an area of small settlement or animal enclosures, houses and cairns on the north from an area where other reeves run at right angles from the main one to the south. One of these subsidiary reeves is roughly, although not precisely, aligned on Hawks Tor, another, the Wotter reeve, on Collard Tor, although again not precisely. The Saddlesborough reeve is actually part of a larger plan, linking up with the Eylesbarrow reeve which lies along the watershed between the Plym and the Meavy Rivers. It is difficult to see this sort of large-scale land division as having taken place in other than open land. Indeed, there are one or two areas where the Eylesbarrow reeve was built in stony land and where it has an irregular course with small curves, as if avoiding individual trees, the implication being that clearance of stones and trees went on together. The tors may have had richer grassland around them due to grazing animals as they and the stone monuments have today (**19, 20**).

15 *Beaver dam and pool with dying trees, St Roman, southern France*

The soils in the area today show a general relation with slope and topography, and the situation was probably similar at the time of the reeves, at least as regards its general diversity if not its detail. Peat overlies rock pavement on the flatter more elevated ground; wet peaty soils (stagnohumic gleys) are also associated with higher elevations and flatter areas; less wet but still peaty soils (ironpan stagnopodzols and ferric stagnopodzols) occur on the more steeply sloping interfluve shoulders, including areas of stony ground, or 'clitter'; while drier soils (brown podzolics) occur in areas of much lower elevation and less severe aspect. But there is much variation. Thus in a transect south-east from the Saddlesborough hillcrest, there is increasing drainage impedence at lower altitudes, with stagnopodzols at the top (c974ft), humic (peaty) gley podzols on the slope (958-935ft), and stagnogleys with thin peat at 925ft at the junction with the Wotter Common reeve (**21**).

Pollen analysis of soils beneath the reeves and blanket peat and of valley peat on and around the moor has shown that there was woodland regeneration and then renewed clearance in the third millennium, before the reeves were built. There was small-scale distribution of heather (*Calluna*), alder (*Alnus*), hazel (*Corylus*) and grassland as an irregular patchwork which mapped the soils. Looking south-east from the hill down the future course of the Saddlesborough reeve just before it was built, there was open hazel scrub which was light-green with yellow catkins (and pale wood) on the drier soils; there was a variegated area of lighter grassland and darker heathland beyond; and then, about

16   *Beaver dam and pools in a backwater of the River Bez, southern France*

17   *A stump and tree felled by beaver, showing the teeth marks*

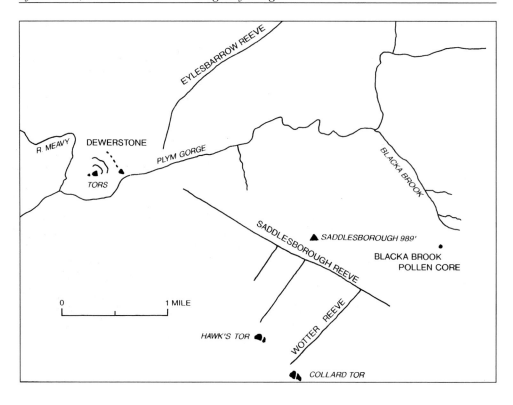

18   Shaugh Moor, Dartmoor. (Based on Smith et al. 1981)

550yds further on, there was an area of alder which was dark-green with red catkins (and dark wood) on the wetter, peatier ground. The alder trees were especially distinctive (**22**). Southwards, along the future line of the reeves to Hawks Tor and Collard Tor there were areas of trodden green grassland around the tors (**19**) and trees growing on them, perhaps of oak and mountain ash.

So before the reeves were built, there was much fine detail of hydrology, soils, vegetation, peaty and stony areas, animal distributions and planned alignments on tors which were not to be precise. Each patch had its own ecosystems and its own phenomenology. Interactions took place between the patches both at the edges — for example birds of prey like kestrels hunting along the edges of woodland — and more widely through human and animal movements across them — as with the territories of lynx, red deer and the domestic animals of man. People moved their animals, from grassland around the tors, through the woodland, to the beaver meadows in the river valleys, probably herding them with dogs. Cattle and sheep may have been intensively used and managed, domestic pigs may have been virtually feral, returned to as needed or used casually, while deer and aurochs were hunted. As materials and energy were moved from one patch of land to another the biophysical environments of the patches and their edges changed. As people met, conversed and crossed the land, as one locality gave way to another, meanings were slightly changed too.

19   Dartmoor showing two standing stones, reeves with heather, and grazed grassland around the tor

The land was organised but this was an arcane organisation, one of knowledge and learning, one that had to be acquired and then thought about. It was as much in people's minds as in the land. The building of the reeves and the formal partitioning of land and settlement did not change any of this in principle. Even though they were very low and unlikely to have supported hedges there were still interactions going on along them. Thus wooden stakes and earth banks were often the first stages in construction, followed by the placing of large stones in a line and then the dumping of piles of small stones around these large ones as land was progressively cleared and used. Infilling of large areas of land by subsidiary reeves took place, and there was soil movement against these boundaries which needed maintaining. Indeed the reeves probably enhanced exchanges in that there were more boundaries. But they brought order and made things more formal, and they subverted — as they perhaps were meant to — the freer-flow of information and the flexibility of the previous state of affairs. People did not need to think so much. Yet it may have been that this control enabled a deeper significance to the interactions which went on within society: in the constriction of freedom, meanings were more fully explored.

Ultimately the reeves extended around the periphery of Dartmoor, and similar massive land enclosure took place in other parts of the British Isles like in Wessex, the East Anglian fen-edge **(p. 41)**, Lincolnshire and north Mayo. Control is a general property of people, as we all know from our everyday lives — on the roads, in work, in the park with the dogs, at home. It can be formalised and institutionalised from above as a part of the power of individuals or priestesses, as is intuitively likely in the case of the reeves with their wide distribution, uniformity of layout and practical futility. Or it can come from within, like

20   *Dartmoor showing short, trampled, grass sward around a standing stone*

the Internet, which is strangely similar to the reeves in being widespread, controlling and an enhancement of information exchange.

There still remain the questions of 'Why reeves?' and 'Why the third millennium BC?' specifically. There are other ways of control such as changes in kinship structure, the more formal use of dogs for herding, burning land, or enhancing the importance of cattle by improving their coats by feeding them barley. Reeves, however, are linear and physical. They were also quite new. This was a time of increasing contrasts at a large scale, and while the diversity in the future reeve area was small-scale it still constituted a significant block of land. The moorland higher up, with its extensive swathes of grassland, heath and blanket peat, was becoming wilder while the woodland or enclosed land lower down was becoming more tamed. The increasing domestication of some animals entailed the increasing wildness of others; whereas in earlier times wolves had been tolerated for their companionship, by the time people were keeping other domestic animals they were much more a threat and may themselves have been hunted. So it may be that the reeves were built to bring this boundary area of Dartmoor, with its ragged diversity of land and restless behaviour, into line with the more structured state-of-affairs elsewhere.

The East Anglian fen-edge

The East Anglian fen-edge is an area of diversity and change and in this it is similar to the zone around the edge of Dartmoor where the reeves were built. But in its specific habitats and niches it is quite different. The area is a boundary of dryland and wetland. It is also

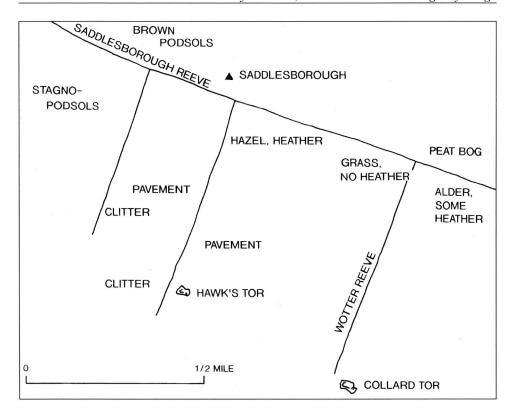

21   *Reeves on Shaugh Moor in relation to tors, soils and vegetation.*
        (Based on Smith et al. *1981; Balaam* et al. *1982)*

a conjunction of the river-valley sequences of soils and alluvium entering the Fenland basin from the western limestone hills and the Fenland sequences of freshwater peats and estuarine and saltmarsh clays deriving from The Wash to the east. The deep sequences in the middle of the fen-basin can be quite straightforward and it is tempting to use these as a framework for discussion. But this would be a serious mistake because it imposes a determinism and regionalism which relate to only one part of the human niche and which may otherwise be irrelevant. Good archaeological sites are usually in areas where the deposits are thinning out at the edges of valleys or the fen so they are not always those with the clearest expression. But it is these with which we should deal.

At Peacock's Farm at the south-east fen-edge in Cambridgeshire, 6 miles west-north-west of Ely, human hunters made visits to a sandy promontory overlooking a tributary of the Great Ouse (**23**). The land was very flat, the top of the sand being only -0.33ft OD, so that promontories and isolated hills, which are in fact irregularities of the fen-edge, stood out in spite of their low height. The river courses that ran among the sandhills and promontories contemporary with the human occupation consisted of tightly meandering main channels and a myriad of finer dendritic ones like the pattern of blood vessels on a lung. Peat began to form in the channels c6660 BC, perhaps as a response to rising water;

22   *Two alder trees,* Alnus glutinosa, *showing distinctive bunching of the growing shoots; around the base of the right-hand older alder elder,* Sambucus nigra, *is growing*

this was the beginning of the Lower Peat of the Fenland sequence. However, the river at the foot of the sand bluff at Peacock's Farm stayed open, if intermittently clogged with peat and vegetation, throughout the occupation.

The hunters first made slight inroads into the dense pine, oak and hazel woodland over two or three centuries from c6500 BC, causing the spread of grasses but little destruction of woodland. More serious impacts, yet still localised ones, took place between c6300-5650 BC, with the area being kept open by burning. Cow-wheat (*Melampyrum*) was present and a thick layer of charcoal formed at the foot of the promontory. Initially just hazel was cleared, perhaps for shelters and other structures. Then pine was cleared and this may reflect the wider influence of fire. Erosion of soil from the promontory suggests disturbance of vegetation, and the increase in grass pollen may reflect opening of vegetation on the promontory and in the wetlands.

All this activity was during short-stay visits. We do not need to suggest directed woodland clearance and the use of fire in it; settlement, casual burning of undergrowth to remove cover for adders, small fires for domestic use and signalling, and some lopping could account for the changes. The people camped on the open sand promontory, slightly above the general surrounds, looking out southwards to pine, hazel and oak woodland with some cleared areas of fen, and to other promontories like Plantation Farm where there were other people (**23**). There were no extensive reed swamps between the river channels although fen plants, like reedmace (*Typha* spp.) and bur-reed (*Sparganium* spp.), and pondweeds (*Potamogeton*) were present. There was curation of flint, as seen in the presence of only a few cores and only one heavy duty pick and the absence of woodworking tools and axes. There was flint microlith manufacture on site and hunting. The top of the promontory is 20ft above the course of the river which is at the bottom of a steep slope, so the immediate location and the general complexity of the river channels would have made it suitable for driving and trapping game; domestic dogs were present by this time and could have been trained for this. The sand promontory at Peacock's Farm was known, permanent and returned to time after time. Yet it never seems to have been more than a focus for small-scale activity. It was not used as a meeting place for people coming from wide areas, although the reduction in pine woodland may reflect wider influence for it outlasts the occupation.

We could propose wider patterns of land-use in which other niches like the developing woodland and reedswamps of the fens, the dry woodlands of the limestone uplands, the broader river valley bottoms and gravel-side terraces, and the coastal saltmarsh and mudflats were brought into an annual round. We could propose responses by humans to changes in woodland cover, in coastal configurations, and in the loss of grazing lands as sea-level rose, perhaps of a demographic kind and being signalled in increasing group identity through increases in the diversity of artefact style. But perhaps this is more about satisfying our needs for order and causal relationships than about the ways in which the Peacock's Farm hunters made decisions about what to do. Immediate lives were about killing the dog that got into their food, moving sharp flint fragments from the campsite, arguing about who was going to carry the baby when they moved, and where to bury the dog. Small struggles over such business were played out in decisions about larger issues like which particular area of saltmarsh to visit this winter.

Long after occupation had ceased at Peacock's Farm, woodland of oak, lime and alder grew up in damp ground with pools (**24**), c5160 BC, which gave way ultimately, as the water-level rose, to reedswamp in alder woodland 2960-2570 BC. Brackish-water Fen Clay began to form shortly afterwards.

The fen-edge is not a simple edge from dryland to fen but is made up of islands, promontories and deep irregular embayments. Sand and gravel make up the main raised ground and there were rivers running through these areas. Before the rise of water-table and the growth of the Lower Peat there was a dry land-surface, a mineral soil and woodland. We saw a bit of this at Peacock's Farm. Further to the north, in the fens north-east of Peterborough, in Morris Fen, Newborough Fen and the Eye peninsula, this surface was colonised by hunters and early farmers who left their flint tools there, especially on the drier, raised, areas (**25**). Minute flint fragments indicate that working of flint was taking place on these areas.

Micromorphology of the argillic brownearths under the Lower Peat shows a complex sequence of change:

1. Illuviation (downwashing) under lime and oak woodland led to the formation of oriented clay coatings on the soil peds (or crumbs) and in the pores; although limpid (clear) these contained fragments of organic matter and charcoal (a condition known as 'dusty'), probably from forest fires (**p. 28**)

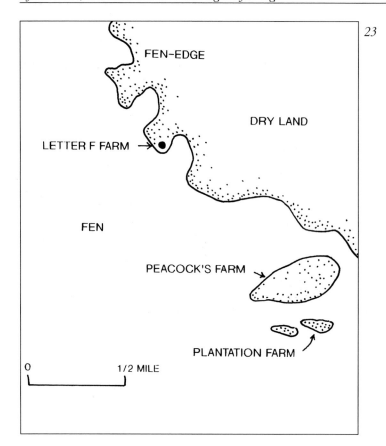

23 *Peacock's Farm and other sites at the fen edge. (Based on Smith et al. 1989)*

2. There was an increase in these coatings as a result of increased illuviation during woodland opening.

3. Further woodland opening and tree-throw led to the illuviation of impure clay and organic matter, fragments of oriented clay from previous soil, and fine sand infilling channels in the soil.

4. Layered fabrics and successions of dusty clay coatings from at least three successive episodes of soil disturbance then formed.

5. Ultimately there was truncation of the soil due to flooding and successive wetting and drying, and its burial as the lower peat began to form.

This work has been done by Charly French. It may be technical but, like the similar work of Peter Moore on upland pre-peat soils **(p. 28)**, it is vital. It is at this level, in the soils, that changes were initiated and where they can be detected. Clearly, there was considerable activity. In the hollow areas between the islands, groundwater rise led to the formation of peat, killing trees and preserving their stumps. Reedswamp and then fen formed although it is not clear whether this showed the zonation we see today around water or whether the different habitats were intermingled. Human use like coppicing, reed cutting, the grazing of animals and woodland management **(p. 84)** may all have been going on. The raised areas were used as focal points for working flint, as hunting stands and lookouts, and perhaps for bigger meetings of several groups.

24   *Reed-swamp and alder spreading into a shallowing lake, as may have occurred at Peacock's Farm after the hunters had left*

Burning issues

Fire has been raised in discussion for three areas — Waun Fignen Felen, Dartmoor and Peacock's Farm — and in broadly hunter-gatherer contexts. It was proposed as far back as 1962 by G.W. Dimbleby that burning may have led to soil change and heathland and blanket peat formation, and that these burnings may have been caused by early hunters. Since then, many kinds of ecological effects and many strategies have been attributed to burning such as an early and abundant presence of hazel after the Ice Age, a sudden spread of alder owing to removal of blocking pine woodlands by burning, the creation of heathland from birch woodland, the creation of small temporary clearings in which fire-resistant herbs and shrubs were present for a short time, the maintenance of particular vegetations especially heathland over longer periods, the maintained rejuvenation of vegetation when burning is repeated, and its role in soil deterioration and blanket peat formation.

Human intent is often ascribed to these burnings, largely on the basis of the circumstantial evidence of associated archaeology, but sometimes on the basis of the charcoal layers and vegetational changes alone **(p. 51)** and a correlation of maintained levels of the same species with charcoal **(p. 25)**. Ethnography, usually from North America, provides strong support, while fire is still used in these islands to rejuvenate heather moors for grouse shooting and purple moorgrass (*Molinia caerulea*) and gorse (*Ulex europea*) for sheep-grazing. On the other hand, an association of burning with climatic dry periods could argue caution in ascribing it to humans.

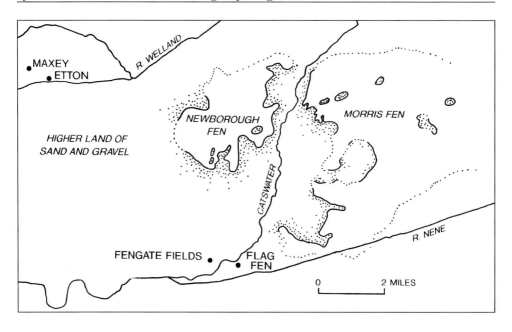

25   *The western fen-edge, with gravel islands in Newborough and Morris Fens. (Based on French 1988)*

But the question of intent is probably unanswerable. More relevant is that fire was a significant part of ecology and was seen as such by human communities. It was there, it was exploited. Certain areas were more susceptible to burning than others because of wind patterns, local topography and hydrology and these would be the areas which people used for the consequences of fire if it suited them. There were many strategies for its use ranging from mainstream intensivity and structured integration with land-use, through casual or marginal use in mobile or opportunistic schemes as and when needed or just when encountered, to even just fiddling around with it at the edge of a settlement or clearing. It was probably used, too, as a reflection of personal or group expression.

The Welland Valley

To the west of the Peterborough fen-edge, in the Welland Valley (**25**), aerial photography has revealed a series of old river channels. They date from between 8950 and the second millennium BC. Some were meandering, some braided, others anastomosing; but whatever the pattern they provided a far greater diversity of land and water than is present in the Welland Valley today.

Archaeological monuments were located in relation to some of these channels (**26**). The Etton causewayed camp, of the later fourth millennium BC, was positioned on the inside of a meander, which, although ultimately eroding into it, may have served as an outer, if only partial, ditch. Another enclosure, Etton Woodgate, was located on similarly low ground but on the opposite site of the river and perhaps using the higher ground of Maxey Island instead of the river as a focus. Much smaller circular ceremonial or burial

26   *Monuments in the*
      Welland Valley; the
      old river course is
      cross-hatched.
      (Based on French
      1990)

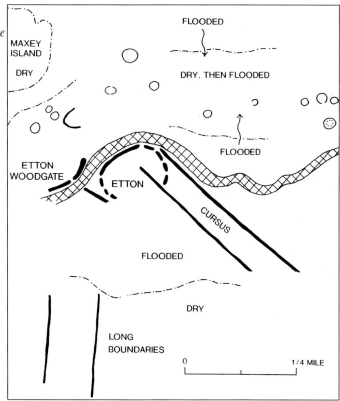

sites were positioned on the slightly higher ground to the north of these two enclosures on the slopes of Maxey Island. The Etton and Maxey Cursuses ran south-east linking two channel belts across another gravel island and to the north-west across Maxey Island to the main Welland floodplain. Although not all of these sites and river channels were in use or active at the same time, it is hard not to imagine that there was integration in their layout, use and meaning.

This area is beyond the Fenland sequence so there is no covering of peat. Environmental evidence comes again from micromorphology and the situation in the fourth-second millennia BC is summarised by French. Soil types and land-use can be related to slight height differences. Areas of lower ground had brownearths since clay illuviation cannot take place under the conditions of wetness which obtain in these locations, while on drier ground like Maxey Island, at 1.6 to 6.5ft higher, there were more mature argillic brownearths. Etton was built on land which had been cleared of woodland and was intermittently flooded, even though it was on a very low island; later in the fourth millennium there were bushes growing in the ditches and alluviation of silt and clay in incremental — possibly seasonal — floodings over the site as a whole. The stream channel skirting the adjacent site of Etton Woodgate was becoming infilled with fine alluvium, and this material and its deposition may have originated from soil disturbance through woodland clearance and agriculture on the higher grounds. The dryland of Maxey Island allowed the building of the henges and barrows there and the cursus which traversed it.

27   *A simple arrangement of gates for controlling and sorting sheep*

Slightly later there was flooding and alluviation on the edges of Maxey Island in areas where other henges and round barrows were soon to be built. (All these slight alluviations are quite separate from the major alluviation in the Welland Valley of the Middle Ages.) The whole area saw spatial and seasonal variation of flooding and alluviation and changes of channel positions during the period when cereals and domestic cattle and sheep were beginning to be used, around 3850 to 3050 BC.

Slightly south to the fen-edge at Fengate (**25**), on a flood-free gravel terrace of the River Nene and Cat's Water, there was substantial settlement and funerary use in the fourth and third millennia BC. Then, during the later part of the third millennium, somewhat earlier than the Dartmoor reeves although continuing in use contemporaneously with them, the land was split up into rectangular areas by ditches and low banks. These were sited at right-angles to the river courses or fen-edge, and the dry ground was linked to the wetter land of the floodplain by double-ditched droveways. But there was no enclosure of the land which was subject to flooding. Pollen analysis indicates that the enclosed land on the higher, drier, ground was pasture, and that the unenclosed land of the valley bottom was flood-meadow with areas of reedswamp. It was first suggested that the Fengate fields were for cattle but Francis Pryor, who has done much of the work on these, now favours a use for sheep farming. At the corners of many of the fields there were gaps and often there had been adjustment or refurbishment of the layout; hurdles could have been sited to change the layout and so could dogs and people. The constructions of double- and triple-ditched boundaries or tracks, with their varying widths and complex junctions of bends and gaps, are seen as stockyards where sheep were inspected, treated and sorted. The process may have been simple, perhaps involving just one farmer (**27**), or more elaborate, with several communities being involved (**28**). Either way it provided a focus for interactions, 'a social landscape of culling, inspection and exchange — embedded within wider social ties and obligations'.

28   A complex arrangement of gates and fences for controlling and sorting sheep

Land and archaeology relations

The land and time diversity of the lower Welland and Nene Valleys and the Fens to the east and south is quite subtle. This is seen in the movements of stream courses, the promontories and islands of the fen-edge, and the reflection of these in different soils and the patchwork of woodland, open dryland and wetland as the water-table rose. Alluviation smoothed out this diversity at the fen-edge but this was countered by the increasing wetness of lowlying land. In a way, things were similar to Dartmoor with a land which was patterned even before there were any human constructions like causewayed camps. It is easy and attractive to see some of the numerous gravel islands, or alternatively the hollow areas and the river meanders, as providing foci for activities of several families or larger groups which were later formalised in the building of the causewayed camps. The rectangular fields brought order and control, like the reeves of Dartmoor, in a boundary zone between the increasingly monotonous fens and the predictability of the drier gravels and limestone uplands.

In this chapter I have looked at hunter-gatherers of the earlier part of the Holocene, and from three areas where there is good evidence of past vegetation and environment. This has been followed up in two of the areas with a look at the ways in which later, farming, communities interacted through their environments. I have shown how there were many small spatial interactions and that these were as much expressions of individual and group control as they were about the practical business of living. Patterns of seasonal movements in regional schemes are eschewed for a more casual order. In ecological changes like the growth of blanket peat and the effects of fire, the emphasis has been on interactions between people and land rather than causation, something that we take up again in later chapters.

4 North-east Ireland to the Shetlands

Lakes and tufa

We start again with lakes. The marls of many lakes are formed by a group of Blue-green Algae (or cyanophytes) called the stoneworts (Characeae). They are named as such because they precipitate calcium carbonate, often as reefs in shallow and well-lit waters around the edge of the lake (**29**). This can be seen in the partially infilled basin at Ballydugan, Co. Down (**33**), where there was a reef of marl rich in Characeae around the edge of the basin, with the central hollow filled in with organic mud. The Burren in Co. Clare, western Ireland, has many such lakes where marl still forms, and when you row over them the change from warmth and light to depth and blackness is uncanny. Interestingly, the Algae can concentrate calcium carbonate and precipitate it as marl even in areas that are not especially lime-rich. Ultimately, the Characeae are succeeded by more diverse vegetation of higher plants (higher on the evolutionary scale, that is) and organic mud and peat form. This may be part of the hydrosere from clear, poor-water, conditions to murky, rich-water, conditions. But it may be related to more general changes in land vegetation and soils and their influence on water and atmospheric chemistry, for, although the marls have been forming from around 14 kya, the main period of growth was during a much narrower interval, from c13 to 9 kya.

The formation of another kind of calcareous precipitate, tufa (**30**), took place mainly during later millennia, from around 6000 to 4000 BC, although again there is a wider range. Here, too, changes in atmospheric carbon dioxide concentrations, soils and vegetation may have been responsible for this pattern. Tufa often forms as reefs in streams where the water is flowing fastest and conditions for algal growth best. The effect is often to dam the streams and create large ponds and openings in woodland, with fallen branches and other vegetation being incorporated into the dams. This is going on in small streams in the Vale of Glamorgan, South Wales, today. Tufa also forms subaerially in wooded swamps, and again this leads to openings in the woods.

The distinction between lake marl and tufa is not absolute because the processes of formation all involve biogenic precipitation by Blue-green Algae; it is more the contexts — lake, stream, subaerial — that differ. Importantly, both these types of deposit lock up concentrations of calcium carbonate which can be released by quarrying and used as fertiliser (**p. 62**) or building stone (**p. 65**).

29   *Stoneworts encrusting reed stems at the edge of Lough Feeney, Co. Clare*

Raised beaches, shell mounds and tombs

In the area of the Ballydugan Lake, in the valleys of the Blackstaff and Quoile Rivers, there are several other lakes. These lie in an isthmus between Dundrum Bay and Strangford Lough which defines the Lecale Peninsula (**31, 32**). Around c6500 BC the isthmus was flooded by brackish water and some of the lakes became partially saline. Estuarine clays with shells and brackish-water deposits infilled the lake basin, directly overlying lacustrine muds (**33**). By c5400 BC this transgression of the sea was well underway.

More widely, in several parts of north-east Ireland, shorelines and beach shingle of this marine transgression occur today at c25ft above sea-level (and higher) because the land has risen since they were formed (**31**). The beach was settled by people from an early stage, and the traces of these settlements are widespread. When the beach was active it was used by people who were exploiting the coastal resources of shellfish and fish. Later on, c4000-2000 BC, when it had risen away from the influence of the sea, its rich soils were attractive to farmers.

Likewise, on the other side of the Irish Sea in south-west Scotland, there are raised beaches of similar origin and these, too, have associated archaeology. In the southern Inner Hebridean islands of Islay, Colonsay, Oronsay and Jura (**34**), the maximum transgression of the sea was c5400 BC although there were significant local variations. On Islay, flint beach pebbles, especially on the west coast, were the main source of stone for tools at this time, although many sites were not directly associated with the contemporary shore. Some were suitable places for watching, stalking and hunting red deer from; one may have been for exploiting freshwater fish from a loch and is also close to the west coast flint; and one was ideal for exploiting wild fowl, presumably in winter. On Colonsay, Staosnaig is

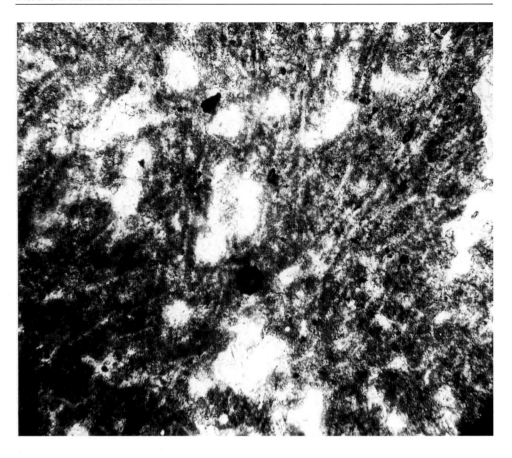

30   Section of tufa showing algal filaments. Width of frame = 1.1 mm

on raised-beach deposits, although these belong to an earlier transgression not associated with the settlement. The site is important since there was intensive use of hazel nuts and their possible storage, a possible hut and a possible burial. There are peculiar elongated artefacts on these sites, usually of stone pebbles but sometimes of bone or red deer antler, which have been artificially bevelled or rounded at one end **(p. 79)**. They may have been used for grinding the seeds of the sand-dune lyme grass (*Elymus arenarius*) to make flour as people did until recently in Iceland.

Oronsay is a very small island, just over 2.5 by 1.9 miles (**34**). It was smaller still at the time of higher sea-levels, with a peculiar tripartite shape, and cut off from the adjacent larger island of Colonsay. On the island there are middens of marine shells and some mammal and bird bones which date from c5250 to 4150 BC. They are close to or on the raised beach, and at one of them the midden material was deposited contemporaneously with the beach. Other middens are underlain by blown sand, a deposit made up of tiny marine shells, foraminifera and other calcareous matter blown onto the land during neap tides. Land snails in the sand below the Cnoc Coig midden indicate open dune prior to midden formation with woodland close by, while pollen from a bog in the north of the

31   Areas dealt with in
chap. 4.
M = Morton

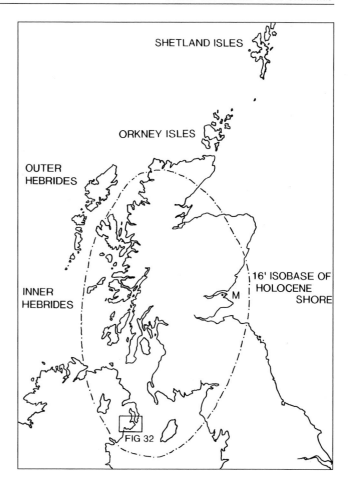

island suggests that the woodland was of hazel and alder, with some oak and birch. So it was all quite diverse. Land snails in blown sand associated with a hunter-gatherer site on the east coast at Morton (**31**) also indicate an environment of woodland at this time.

The shell mounds on Oronsay are true middens, being the dumps of material from activities elsewhere, although there are some hearths in them, especially in Cnoc Coig, indicating a variety of uses. They probably represent occasional settlement by small groups or individuals over long periods of time since they are quite small, at 95ft across, and contain few artefacts. The occasional mammal bones include fur-bearers like otter, pine marten and weasel, and food animals, rorqual, small cetacean (?dolphin), red deer, wild pig and grey seal, with red deer antler being used for artefacts. There are also a few human bones, especially of hands and feet. Fish bones of saithe are abundant and the ear-bones allow season of catch to be identified, here showing that each of the five middens was occupied at a quite specific and slightly different time of the year, as if used by a separate group. But the bulk of the middens is made up of limpet shells packed together, some dogwhelks and a few other species like scallops. There were distinctive bone and red deer antler barbed missile heads which may have been for spears or leisters, there were bevelled artefacts, there were bone and antler awls, and there were antler mattocks.

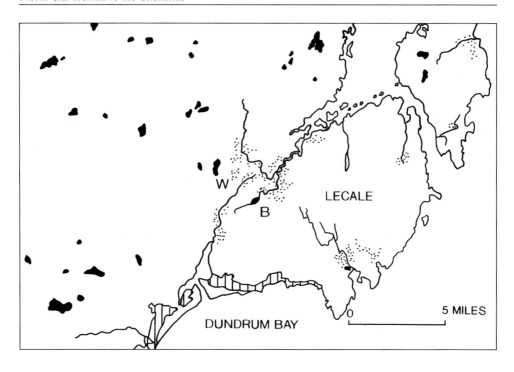

32   *Lecale, Co. Down (31). Vertical hatching = terrace of Holocene raised beach; stippling = alluvium; black = lakes; B, Ballydugan; W, Woodgrange. (Based on Singh & Smith 1973)*

Other sites with similar cultural affinities are the islet of Risga in Loch Sunart, a series of small cave middens, quite unsuitable for permanent occupation, around Oban on the mainland coast, and a cave on the island of Ulva off the coast of Mull (**34**). Many of the features of these sites, including their small size, their unsuitability for permanent occupation, the task-specific activities, the narrow resource base (in spite of the numerous mammals species), and the long duration but only seasonal nature of occupation, suggest that people were coming to them for solitude or privation. They may have been hermits, or shamans, or youths undertaking rites of passage. The association of shell-middens and raised beaches may, then, have been more than a functional one. It may have created a perception of the coast as a liminal zone, with movement across it needing negotiation through the middens, perhaps enhanced through the burial of human remains in them. Indeed, it might be better to use a more neutral word for the middens, like shell-mound, if they were created with a future use in mind, since 'midden' has such implications of disposal and finality. The term 'liminal' also needs thought, strictly referring to the locality, to your point of view, not to the locale of the coast *per se*. Liminality was constituted in the exchanges and negotiations that took place as you moved past the shell mounds in whichever direction. There was a feeling of tension before the zone was crossed which afterwards gave way to relief.

If, then, these small coastal cave and island sites were about privation, of whatever sort, this has significance for how people viewed and presented themselves. Privation

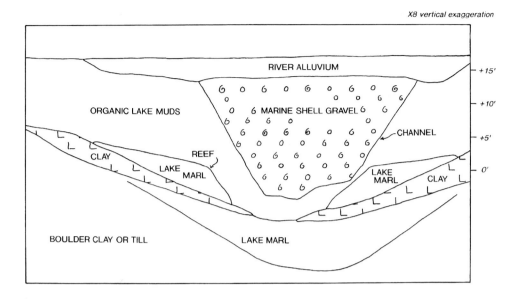

X8 vertical exaggeration

33   Section through deposits at Ballydugan (32). (Based on Singh & Smith 1973)

or eremitism implies an understanding of social obligations and, indeed, perhaps a greater understanding of them than by people who live in communities. Sociability is a fundamental manifestation of humanity, and a need to avoid it may be at the heart of these small middens. At the same time, their seasonality implies that this was not a permanent, Trappistinic, withdrawal and that the people involved returned every so often to their communities where they could have imparted the wisdom of their thoughts.

Shell mounds on the west coast were also relevant to later communities. Exposure of raised beaches and the fertile lands on them in the fifth and fourth millennia BC may have been rapid, perhaps around 4-6ft vertical per century, and in flat areas people would have noticed this. Valuable grazings and arable land became available and access to these needed to be negotiated. This could have been done through the interfacing of new-style chambered tombs with the shell mounds of the past. The tombs were sometimes sited over the shell mounds, perhaps to cancel out their power or perhaps to legitimate changes in land-use by newcomers through the past. So the locations and distribution of chambered tombs, like those on Arran, must be seen in relation to these historical factors as well as to more conventional ones of agricultural land and areas for deer-hunting.

Outside the areas of the raised beach

In the Outer Hebrides, parts of the Scottish mainland, Orkney and Shetland, coastal sites have been eroded by the sea because there has been no protection through uplift (**31**). There has, however, as in the raised beach areas, been some preservation under blown sand, and indeed erosion and preservation have gone on as part of the same general process.

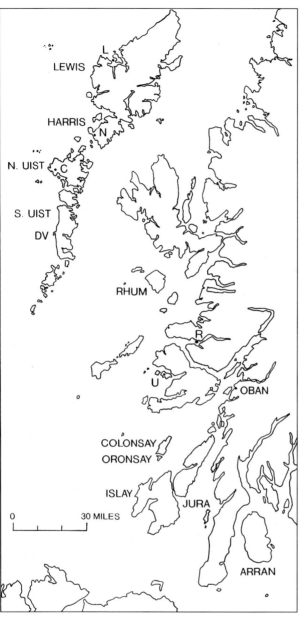

34   *Sites mentioned in chap. 4.*
C, Clettraval;
DV, Dun Vulan;
L, Loch na Bierie;
N, Northton;
R, Risga;
U, Ulva

For hunter-gatherers and the earliest farmers, before the influence of blown sand, there was non-calcareous soil supporting hazel and birch woodland, although this was often cleared locally. The earliest deposition of blown sand, perhaps as early as 4000 BC, may have taken place in woodland and was usually slight, not sufficient to kill the vegetation. In fact it actually made the soil more fertile, and this may have been one of the reasons for the success of the early agricultural settlements in the Outer Hebrides and Orkney. Away from the immediate influence of the sea and the blown sand, peatlands and heaths started to form as early as 7600/7000 BC, with an increase in rate and spread c3000/2500

BC. Initially peat formation enhanced the diversity of the land, perhaps breaking up the woodland and introducing alternative resources for fuel, building materials, bedding and grazing. In the areas of both blown sand and peat formation, the interplay and timing of the processes that led to deforestation, such as increasing influence of salt spray and storms, destruction by people, burning, soil acidification and burial by sand and peat themselves, are unknown. But what is crucial is the diversity of land offered by these early periods of change.

Later on, the deposits became more extensive and thicker and the earlier diversity was lost. Thus from 3550 BC, and especially on west coasts where there are extensive flat, low-lying lands, blown sand formed over many tens of square miles. It was even blown up valleys to considerable heights, spreading onto acid soils and peat. These lands, often calcareous and usually stabilised by vegetation, are known as 'machair', and since the sands increase the fertility of the land, they were widely used for agriculture. In bays and estuaries, the blown sand and coastal storm beaches blocked river drainages and led to the formation of freshwater lochs or brackish lagoons, with extensive sedge fen and reedswamp (**35**). Camps and homesteads were sited at the edges of these wetlands in prehistory, and when they were adjacent to growing peat or accumulating sand these settlements had access to a huge diversity of habitats. Beyond the machair towards the sea were the active foredunes and storm beaches, and beyond these again the low-tidal mud-flats and sandy shores where species of shellfish like oysters, cockles and razorshells, which were specifically adapted to these habitats, lived. These were often collected by the inhabitants of the machair and taken to their settlements.

In South Uist in the Outer Hebrides, the machair of the lowlying western side of the island is particularly well-developed. There are land surfaces with soil horizons below and within the machair and these were settled at various times, although not before c3550 BC, and then from the start by farming communities; only blips of charcoal and clearance episodes in the pollen diagrams suggest a pre-farming presence. Some of the settlements show today as low mounds, while others are visible in coastal erosions, and teams from Cardiff and Sheffield Universities are studying these. The mounds are made up of the foundations of stone buildings, hearths, floors, some metal-working areas, abundant refuse of pottery, shells and animal bone, and successive layers of blown sand. The earliest ones were irregularly spaced, but the later ones, of the first millennium BC into the first few centuries of the first millennium AD, were more uniformly distributed as if taking up territories in relation to each other. The settlement of the machair and the mounds went on until the later Middle Ages when there was a move to the peaty and mineral soils inland. The stone tower houses called brochs, however, were always sited outside the machair except for a few on coastal headlands.

In settling the machair and adjacent lands, people chose areas for their diversity and fertility. But the areas were inherently changing and there were costs. The sandy soils are susceptible to wind erosion, so topsoil could be lost quickly, while other areas, including settlements, were buried; fresh sand blown from the shore had the same effect; and coastal erosion often led to the destruction of extensive areas of machair, lakes and, again, settlements. Many archaeological sites which are now coastal were once inland, not necessarily far inland, but sufficiently so to have been in different biophysical surrounds

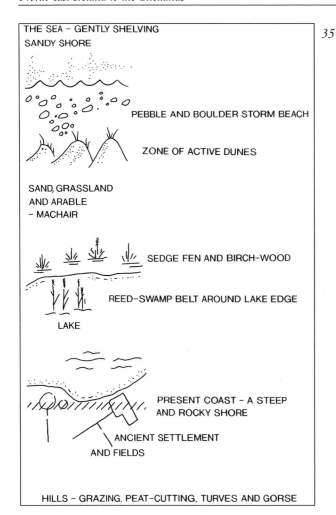

THE SEA – GENTLY SHELVING
SANDY SHORE

PEBBLE AND BOULDER STORM BEACH

ZONE OF ACTIVE DUNES

SAND, GRASSLAND
AND ARABLE
– MACHAIR

SEDGE FEN AND BIRCH-WOOD

REED-SWAMP BELT AROUND LAKE EDGE

LAKE

PRESENT COAST – A STEEP
AND ROCKY SHORE

ANCIENT SETTLEMENT
AND FIELDS

HILLS – GRAZING, PEAT-CUTTING, TURVES AND GORSE

35 *Habitats in a coastal area; the present shore is towards the bottom at the cross hatched band*

(**35**). This is so with the deeply stratified occupation at Northton, South Harris (**34**), and the settlements of early farmers in Orkney, especially Skara Brae on Mainland and Knap of Howar on Papa Westray (**44**). The remains of these settlements can be seen in coastal cliff sections while the deposits of the former lakes appear as peats and shell-beds in the intertidal zone. The molluscs of these steep and rocky shores are winkles, dog whelks and limpets, specifically adapted to such conditions and quite different from the sandy- and muddy-shore species which were collected in earlier times. Buildings of the second and first millennia BC and structures of the historic ages like Viking houses and medieval farm mounds have been similarly affected, with some sites like Eastshore of Virkie on Shetland having been sliced in half by the sea, others completely buried by sand.

Inland, beyond the influence of the blown sand, c1000 BC, there was soil acidification and iron-panning leading to an increase in the spread of peat and *Calluna vulgaris* heathland. In Orkney, from the fourth-first millennia BC, there was a reduction in birch and hazel woodland, as at Loch of Knitchen, Rousay, and Loch of Torness, Hoy (**44**). Ultimately there was a severe reduction in good pasture and woodland; and areas which had been settled and farmed in the fourth-second millennia BC became rough grazing and growing peat. These changes were probably caused by woodland clearance, agriculture and exposure to extreme westerly winds and rain. Burning and grazing may also have been involved, although these, depending on their intensity, could have either retarded peat formation and heather growth by maintaining grassland or accelerated it by causing podsolisation and waterlogging. There was a delicate balance here. Lakes were becoming filled in.

The dwindling of valuable food resources and land as a result of these changes of coastal form, shellfish species and the distribution of lagoons, blown sand and peat, were serious enough to have been noticed. Access squabbles, tenure disagreements especially where there was burial or erosion of soil, and mediation of these through ritual were probably common. As a part of this, Richard Hingley has identified the purposeful and involved reuse of earlier sites, as in the chambered cairns on North Uist and Orkney during the period 800-1 BC, where grave materials, including human bone, were replaced by other materials like pottery. Substantial modification and incorporation of tomb architecture into later structures is also seen in certain brochs in North Uist and Orkney; in the long cairn of Clettraval on North Uist which was incorporated into a wheelhouse; at Howe, Orkney, which was modified into an enclosure; and at Knowe of Rowiegar on Rousay, Orkney, which was incorporated into a souterrain, and where there was direct copying of the architecture of the tomb (**34, 44**).

This may go back even further, as noted by Chris Lowe for the re-use of a funerary focus by a settlement at St Boniface, Papa Westray, c1250 BC. Changing architecture in stone-built settlements of the first millennium BC, especially of enclosures, passages and the development of extra-mural space was relevant in terms of increasing control of personnel and their perceptions of the site. Towards the end of the millennium and into the first millennium AD, poignant examples of ritual are seen in the use of human and animal remains, including the burial of a seated arthritic old man beneath the floor of an enclosure at Crosskirk and of an arthritic cat at St Boniface, significantly just prior to abandonment. At St Boniface, again, there was continuity of ecclesiastical settlement, with some of this perhaps to do with 'the establishment of eremitic groups or individuals on Orkney in the eighth century AD'.

Brochs

Brochs are a striking feature of these western and northern lands and islands. Built during the closing centuries of the first millennium BC and the early centuries of the first millennium AD, these round towers were probably farmsteads. They provide an attractive focus for study because of their monumentality, their idiosyncratic architecture (**37-42**) and their overall compact, yet uneven, distributions (**36**). Yet it is unlikely that they were a dominant influence in any one community and even more unlikely that they provided a unitary and unifying focus over their whole area of distribution. There is regional diversity in siting, in their relation to other house types and in the relationships of the communities who lived in them; there is even debate over whether brochs are a distinct type apart from 'Atlantic roundhouses' at all. And as with all striking monument

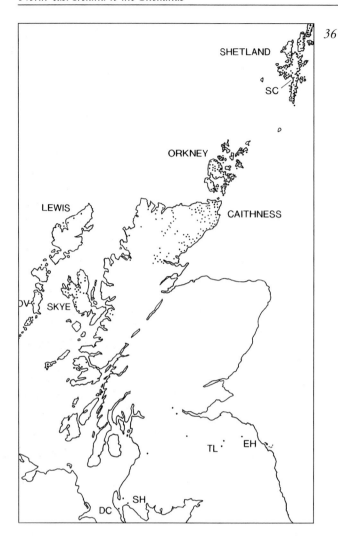

36 Brochs.
DC, Doon Castle;
DV, Dun Vulan;
EH, Edin's Hall;
SC, Scalloway;
SH, Stairhaven;
TL, Torwoodlee

types, brochs could be mere trim, just brief statements in lives that otherwise saw no change from one side of the broch horizon to the other. Still, brochs are distinctive, with shared features from the most southerly in Galloway, to the most westerly in the Outer Hebrides, and the most easterly and northerly in north-east Scotland and the Shetlands, making them unquestionably related. For this reason and because they exemplify other archaeological types with distinctive distributions, we can use them in examining ideas about monuments, land and people.

I am not concerned with origins and spread. It is true that brochs were built in many areas where soil fertility was declining and bog and heath were spreading. Land diversity was becoming reduced and there were increasing extremes of more distinctive and extensive blocks of land like blanket peat, acid heathland and machair. But links between these changes and brochs, as reflecting the hierarchisation of power, concepts of the households, or earlier and now less popular views of immigrants or defence against invaders, are difficult to sustain. There are too many unknown factors of chronology and

37   Staircase in Stairhaven broch

how people related to the land. And there was still much land diversity, and there were still many lakes. I am more interested in looking at relationships which might have arisen within individual communities because of brochs.

Of course, brochs were irrelevant to a lot of behaviour. Personal interactions often took precedence, and for individuals the whole process of growing up and becoming wise may have had nothing to do with the broch. Equally, ideas and their interpretations not only developed in individuals without the influence of the outside world but were selective and reinforcing:

> . . . shamans who know that they are frauds nevertheless also believe in their powers, and especially in those of other shamans: they consult them when they themselves or their children are ill.

A.L. Kroeber, cited in E. Goffman, 1969, *The presentation of self in everyday life*

We believe the part we are playing.

38 *Entrance of Stairhaven broch Galloway, from within. Note the curvature of the entrance passage*

Similarly in communities, information sent out is influenced by manipulation and dissembling, while information received is immediately interpreted. There is a whole structure brought about by discrepancies of communication and presentation before we even come to the broch. There is the similarity we see (or think we do) in dogs and owners and the way in which this is enhanced by other people's perceptions. There are the different groupings of ethnicity, age or activity and the ways these take on meanings beyond the purely physical or biological in terms of the household, of power, or of prejudice. There are the relative contributions of unthought-out practical responses and the deeper synthesis of learning and tradition, and these can vary in their significance according to who you are, where you are in the community, and the occasion.

But there still is the biophysical environment and mostly it is relevant in people's lives. Sociologists have stressed the importance of reflexivity in mediating between people themselves and between people and the biophysical environment — the to and fro of changing perceptions between structure and agency —, and archaeologists have done so with land, architecture and smaller items of material culture. The lives which are continually being reproduced in thinking, behaviour, material culture and communal order, change continuously because of interpretation. And in this reflexivity and change is the creation of localities and their interpretative power. For brochs, each could have a different meaning: at an extreme, the only reality for each and every broch is as an individual one. So while the questions that arise from their idiosyncratic building style are obvious ones, like: 'If brochs are dwellings, which they seem to be, why are they monumental?' or 'What is the purpose of the nuances of architecture like the guard-chambers, the low entrance, and the extreme thickness of the walls?' (**39, 40**), the answers are not so obvious because they are interpretations. Clearly there was an origin for guard-chambers — in the

39   *Entrance of a chamber at Edin's Hall. Note the monolithic step, perhaps to keep out rodents or to emphasise the importance of the gap*

chambers of chambered tombs, a place for idols, dog-kennels or even guarding. And this was known and perpetuated in some brochs. But in others it was lost, the feature surviving as a traditional bit of style, to be constructed variously depending on combinations of personnel and time.

Still, the setting is important. Often you cannot start a particular performance like cooking, mucking out animals, or feasting without a particular setting, however much human agency weights the nature of the locality. Deposits on the ground floor of the broch interior at Scalloway, Shetland, suggested to the excavator, Niall Sharples, that it had been used for stalling cattle during winter; that the entire structure had then been burnt and the used straw and remaining fodder removed in the spring; and that the area had been used for human occupation with pits until the autumn, when the pits were infilled and the area gravelled and paved in preparation for the overwintering of animals again. Human occupation during winter was likely on the first floor of the broch or in buildings elsewhere. It was the same for the middens: they had to come from particular areas and be in particular settings to play their part. At Scalloway, Shetland, and Dun Vulan, South Uist, there were middens to the south of the broch door which had accumulated where domestic and farm materials were dumped away from living areas. At Scalloway it was especially the materials from cleaning out the animal stalls which were in the midden, reflecting the status of the occupants and their control over fertility; kitchen, butchery and metalworking wastes, in contrast, were dumped behind the broch in a ditch. But the middens are at odds with the need for the material to fertilise the fields, so maybe this was less important than their visibility; or perhaps the middens developed late in the life-history of the brochs having lost their use in maintaining the fertility of the arable land

40   *Entrance of Edin's Hall. Note the guard-chambers*

as other means for this were found **(p. 62)** but still retaining their symbolism of status. But all of this, whatever its significance, could only take place within the broch and just outside its entrance.

Brochs held a diversity of these locales **(37-42)**. Yet the area was small and there was little relief from the confinement of both physical space and meetings with people. The contrast between inside and outside was intensive, much more so than in forts where there was always open ground among the buildings in spite of the embankments around them. You can see this in two of the brochs in south-east Scotland, Edin's Hall **(43)** and Torwoodlee, which are inside forts. In the brochs, the self-aggrandisement of the head-person was strengthened by the massive-walled tower, by the low, long and narrow passage to the outside, by the surrounding lesser dwellings, and by the slightly elevated and immune position in the land. The fact that none of this could be physically seen from within the broch enhanced the effect. There was a queen-bee feeling, and indeed the broch head-person may never have left the broch. At Edin's Hall the broch is at the west end of the hillfort, away from and slightly skewed to a long passage through the settlement so that it was not seen when approaching the hillfort until you were inside it. The massive thickness of the walls of the broch may be an attempt to subvert this openness, a sort of metaphorical filling-in of the space between the hillfort banks. It may also have been a psychological strengthening against the self-assurance of outsiders like overlords and tinkers, people who needed no physical setting at all but created their own wherever they went just by being themselves. In contrast, for more lowly people, this physical separation from the outside might have engendered feelings of oppression or defeat while in the

41   Walling inside Edin's Hall

broch, but which were successively released as the building was left — along the passage, past the guard-chambers, stooping low at the interface with the outside, and then . . . daylight and freedom. There is a similar feeling in leaving the chambered tombs of an earlier time, some of which were incorporated into the brochs and in which we might see the origin of this feature. And these feelings of individuals are linked to collective psyches, such as of households, communities and people, and to wider authorities. They are also relative and quite subjective. In the 'broch villages' in Orkney and Caithness, for example, we may feel oppression in the closely-packed houses and yards around the walls outside of the brochs or we may be imbued with a sense of belonging as part of a household hierarchy in which a head and dominant family lived in the broch and the dependent families at the base of the walls outside.

Brochs allowed the creation of yet more localities in the way they related to land. The building process itself was a communal effort involving several families. It entailed organisation of quarries, stone selection and dressing, transportation and engineering of the architecture. When the stone came from earlier settlements, it embodied nature and ancestry and engendered permanence of memory. Importantly the building process was itself an artefact as much as the broch, entailing an expression of social relations at all stages and to which the form of the broch might relate. Siting reflects a function as farmhouses or locations from which farming was organised. In the Shetlands, siting of brochs in relation to each other suggests a pattern of agricultural territories, each of which could have supported a few hundred people. In some areas, again as in the Shetlands, locations may additionally have been related to defence, the coast or sources of building stone. These locales of construction and farming — stone quarries, individual and different fields, their gaps and boundaries, piles of cleared stone and heaps of manure,

42   Entrance of Doon Castle, Galloway, with instepped door

tracks and significant landmarks — were integrated with those of the homestead and allowed the interchange and modification of experiences to take place.

This was enhanced by the ways in which brochs were often at boundaries. Thus a more specific relationship with agricultural land was at the edges of it and away from other settlements, probably so that use of different habitats, like grazing and arable, hay meadow and water, and of different territories could be optimised. It is seen in the two south-western brochs, Edin's Hall and Torwoodlee, both close to grazing land and arable, on the edges of plateaus below higher ground, and just above a steep slope down to a river. There were boundaries, too, with non-broch settlements, as in South Uist, where brochs, in addition to being at the boundary of the white sandy machair and the 'blacklands' of peat and moorland grazing, show a complementarity of distribution with adjacent non-broch settlements which were within the machair. There was also dependency of the broch communities on these other settlements as shown by the high slaughter rate of young animals at Dun Vulan which would have left a herd with an age structure unviable for its maintenance and thus dependent on stock from outside. And there were differences in the food animals between brochs and non-brochs, with broch communities having a more diverse lifestyle, including young pigs and calves, fish, seabirds, seals and red deer.

There were boundaries, too, of time. Cosmology was embedded in entrance orientations, 39% of which (out of a sample of 90) faced more or less to the west,

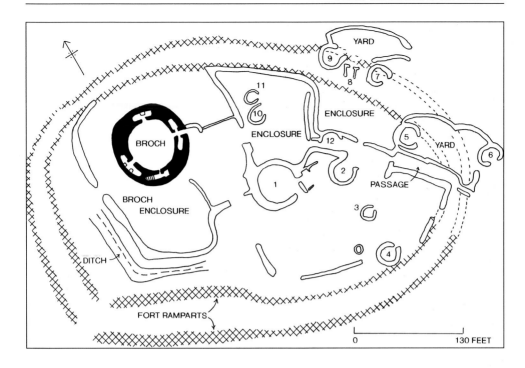

43   *Edin's Hall, broch, fort and settlement; 1 to 12 are huts. (Based on a drawing by Andrew Dunwell, unpublished) Crown Copyright: Historic Scotland*

subverting a more natural tendency of seeing east as front and thus a deliberate demonstration of difference. This present was lived within a land of older farms and even older chambered tombs, some of which were incorporated into the broch fabric, and which, in the appropriation of ancestral power, legitimated this new building form and farming. The future was in the new monumentality and complexity of brochs and the ambitions of their occupants for change.

The various boundary locations of brochs as well as their boundedness themselves, in their uncompromisingly featureless walls and tower and their isolation, often slightly elevated, on promontories or islands, and against a backdrop of wildness, allowed various meanings and functions to be played out both by those within the brochs and those outside. Some sitings, even though close to farmland and the sea, defensible and prominent, are difficult to explain in their perversity. Stairhaven (**37, 38**) and Doon Castle (**42**) are on rocky coastal outcrops which are continued straight up into the broch walls: defence and prestige are obvious explanations, but these could have been achieved just as easily and in locations very close by with much less effort. Doon Castle is extraordinary in being on the end of a narrow ridge with a ravine and then the open sea on one side and a gully on the other. It also has two entrances, opposite each other. It was set within an earlier promontory fort with a deep rock-cut ditch and a bank revetted with stones inside of this. Rights and access to land, legitimation of territory, and mediation of a more sinister role of coercion or brigandage may all have been involved in these places within broader ideas of households or power. And there was an achievement of deep psychological security, especially in the unification with nature.

Life was also lived within a wider world of total broch distribution (36). Although no one community knew its entirety, some general features such as that it was northern, western, peripheral and significantly coastal would have been understood. Awareness was probably made real through talk of traits, customs or material culture rather than bald geographical distributions. Local variations would have been known locally as in the concentrations of brochs in northern Skye and western Lewis, and broch communities at the edge of the major distributions and those which were on their own would have been especially aware of their singular locations. If we must look at regional groupings then these should be in terms of different kinds of community structure in different areas, with different degrees of independence, identity and belief; or of the relative contributions of practical order and social construction both between and within the different communities. The abstract architecture of personal and community relationships can be much stronger, more enduringly structured, and have many more facets from which localities can be created than the concrete architecture of the biophysical surrounds.

Manure

In these western and northern isles there was likely exploitation in an annual or longer round of land-use of different environments — the sea, the coast, the machair, the lagoons and reedswamps, the neutral and acid blacklands, and the uplands of peat and lochs. Where soils were used for agriculture there was an increasing need for their maintenance, and this was met by an integrated use of resources from the different land zones. The cool and wet climate and the high degree of leaching, acidity and waterlogging that this entailed meant that rates of nitrogen fixation and phosphorus mineralisation in the soils were low. Soil fertility was a critical problem, and so was winter-feeding of animals. The coast was often the answer, especially as there was relatively more land for farming near the coast than in other regions of the British Isles and especially on islands where there was relatively more coast to land. Average returns were obtained by spreading animal dung from pasture and meadow onto arable, while increased yields were obtained from a diversity of practices. Thus as arable expanded at the expense of pasture and as there was correspondingly less dung, people transported hill turves, peat, lake marl, shell-sand and seaweed to the arable land, as well as using materials from discarded thatch, turf walls and byres. They brought their animals into the infield after the harvest to feed on the arable stubble, thus enhancing its fertility, a practice called 'tathing'. And they used increasingly intensive techniques of tillage and weeding.

These practices are seen in the deep topsoils around farms in parts of Mainland Orkney, especially the deep top phase of the Bilbster Series, which is more than 2.5ft thick and occasionally up to 3.8ft, and with enhanced phosphate of two or three times the normal levels (44). The soil built up at a rate of c1mm per year during and after the Middle Ages due to manuring, with the main contribution being from turves mucked out from byres. Interestingly, stable isotope analysis shows seaweed not to have been used much in contrast to the evidence of written sources where its importance is stressed, possibly as a bit of propaganda to support a dwindling industry. Soils are noticeably thicker nearest to the farms and this is especially so on the Shetland island of Papa Stour in the contrast between the deep topsoils around the settlements and the impoverished heathland soils beyond the head-dyke. And these contrasts became accentuated as more and more turves for cattle bedding and peat for fuel were taken from beyond the head-dyke and as tathing of animals in the infield intensified.

C-14 dating suggests that deep topsoils were forming from the late twelfth century AD, a time when new settlement names suggest increased agricultural organisation, although an earlier, Norse, origin has also been proposed. At St Boniface they may even be accommodated within an Early Christian chronology, and they are linked to ecclesiastical settlements as on Iona, around Fearn Abbey in Easter Ross, and at St Boniface Church on Papa Westray. But the practices, if not the actual increases in topsoil thickness, probably go back into prehistory, as at Tofts Nest on Sanday, Orkney, from before c3000 BC, where there may also have been management by burning.

A further dimension to all this are the 'farm mounds'. This term, like that of many archaeological monument types, is unfortunate because it encompasses a variety of origins and has led to a focus of discussion around the name itself when attention to function and meaning of individual sites would be more productive. There are many origins of mounds. Bird colonies, especially of seabirds, often occur in areas of increased topsoil thickness, and while this is certainly due to build up of guano, sometimes to exploitable thicknesses, it may also be that the colonies were sited on areas of enhanced topsoil depth in the first place because of their suitability for burrowing. This is likely with the Manx shearwater colonies on the prehistoric fields of Skomer Island off the south-west coast of Pembrokeshire. A mound at St Boniface, Papa Westray, is the waste from a medieval fish-processing factory.

Farm mounds actually associated with farms are particularly common on Sanday and North Ronaldsay in Orkney (44), and originate from at least the time of Norse influence as indicated by placenames and C-14. They formed by the accumulation of the same sort of materials that contributed to the deep topsoils, ash of domestic hearths and bedding material from byres. Apparently, this material was not put on the fields as manure because of the inherent fertility of the calcareous sandy soils of these two islands. But there are other islands with little sand which have farm mounds.

The deep topsoils and farm mounds increased the diversity of the land. In many cases there were lakes close to the farms, and these added to this diversity on quite a small-scale (44). Time management had to be well organised, involving a knowledge of the way in which different areas of land could be used and integrated, especially in the movement around of all the diverse materials and animals from one area to another. Co-operation between different communities over the use of, and access to, different areas of land and animals was necessary, and a highly structured routine was developed.

As well as having obvious practical benefits, of course, this diversity allowed the greater mediation of people's interactions and expression. It increased the number of places where contacts and information transfers could take place and where community bonds were played out. In this, the histories of the land played a part. Thus the farm mounds may have been constructed in the first place not just as a means of storing manure or disposing of

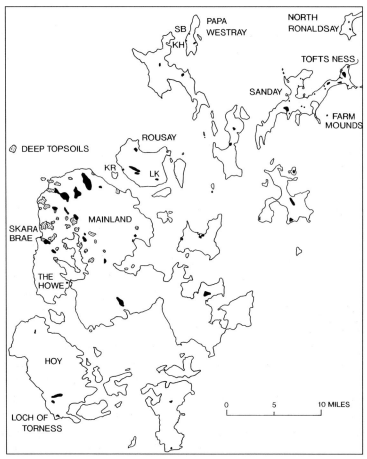

44   *Orkney Islands; lakes shown black. Farm mounds after Davidson* et al. *1986; deep topsoils after Davidson & Simpson 1984.*
KH, Knap of Howar; KR, Knowe of Roweigar; LK, Loch of Knitchen; SB, St Boniface

dung but as symbols of territoriality, access or status, and this could have been enhanced through the use of fertile materials which themselves had come from significant areas and been used for specific purposes. We saw this earlier with the middens outside some brochs. Their later development as striking landscape features, some being over 13ft high, may have strengthened these roles but also deflected them into other ways of meaning. Even the deep topsoils are essentially low mounds and may have been deliberately built up in particular areas and confined to particular activities, not just distributed in the arable land generally.

This chapter has been based on coastal areas of the west and north of the British Isles. It is exemplary of my approach to environmental histories: loosely regional for convenience, and with a sequence which looks at one thing and then takes off from ideas generated by it to another. It is how things happened. Specifically it has been about changing meanings both in relation to different groups of people and histories. This has been explored through the reuse of land, shell mounds and monuments, through brochs, and through the movement of materials and animals in coastal farming communities.

5 Inorganic raw materials

The use of inorganic raw materials by people is a unifying theme because it seems discontinuous in terms of time, space, personnel and itself. It is occasional, it occurs in narrowly circumscribed places, it is done by small sections of communities and it is separate from everyday life. Mining and quarrying were often highly communal and physical, while stone-working, smelting, casting and forging were equally often intensely solitary and arcane. Metal-working, in particular, allowed access to the supernatural. The iron- and bronze-working sites in the rainswept hillforts of the Welsh Marches, like Llwyn Bryn-Dinas, dark and enclosed, evoke isolation, cussedness and wisdom. Organic materials, in contrast, tend to be exploited more widely and continuously and be less divorced from everyday activities, indeed to constitute them. Clearly this is a bit of an over-generalisation when we think about hunting and the use of plants which were often quite localised, but the fact remains that the exploitation of inorganic raw materials is perceived as a more distinctly separate part of life. The invention of metal-working and metal artefacts, especially, entailed radical new practices, as in pyrotechnology and the selective circulation and deposition of artefacts, and it involved a greater awareness of distant lands in people's lives. It led to new divisions and feelings of alienation especially in the areas of greatest specialisation like smelting and casting. It was the start of the separation of people and nature.

In other ways, however, the exploitation of inorganic raw materials was not separate from the normal business of life. There was an embeddedness of meaning in all its aspects — the siting of places for extraction, the extraction processes themselves, the distribution and working of the raw materials, metals and weapons, and their use and ultimate deposition. For example, at Lydney in Gloucestershire (**47**), a Roman temple complex on a promontory overlooking the River Severn is sited within an earlier, prehistoric, fort and is associated with the shafts of iron-ore extraction. Some of the stones of the temple are tufa, a spring deposit **(p. 44)**, which is significant as a metaphor of birth; a bronze statuette of a dog was found in the Roman levels (**45**), which may be significant, supposedly in terms of a healing cult; and mistletoe grows on a tree at the fort entrance (**46**), which is probably not significant — although it does show the strikingly visible impact that this semi-parasite could have given had it been there in the past.

At a wider level, Richard Hingley sees a metaphorical integration of iron, ironworking and the re-use of scrap and hoards with biological birth, life, death and re-birth. The conversion of stone to metal and the use of metal for such emotive and economically central tools as ploughshares and swords are clear analogues of animal and human death and regeneration. As John Barrett and Stuart Needham have written: bronze-working

45   *Bronze statuette of a Roman dog from Lydney, Gloucestershire; note the collar and the extremely long snout. Length of statuette, 4 ins. (With permission of Viscount Bledisloe, Lydney Estate)*

and bronzes were a part of the total life system, with production not on the fringes but integrated with cycles of agriculture and consumption and having deeply embedded significances for everyone. And in the political sphere, leaders in the first millennium BC in southern Britain drew on these metaphors and actualities of the farming year — the combined ability to kill and bestow fertility — in their implementation of authority.

Sources

There are instances where extraction went on more or less continuously at a low level of intensity, especially where embedded in other activities like skinning and butchery. This was often the case in earlier periods of prehistory where flint was collected from beaches and collapsed cliffs **(p. 13)**, and it was probably one of the reasons why these people liked coasts and rivers. Exploitation was done by local people locally. Metal ores too could be collected from the surface, as was the practice with iron ores in the later part of the first millennium BC over much of southern England, perhaps while people worked the arable fields.

But many sources were more localised. Several kinds of foreign stone, some perhaps from north Devon, were used at Paviland by Ice-Age hunters in the third decachiliad **(p. 18)**. Rhum bloodstone, Arran pitchstone and Portland chert were used by hunter-gatherers in the sixth millennium BC **(47)**. Specific sources of igneous and metamorphic rocks in the west of Britain were used by farming communities from the fourth millennium onwards, and during the same period, there was mining of flint in southern England from seams in chalk. Stone for large constructions was usually of local origin, with the formidable exception of the Stonehenge sarsens from the Marlborough

46 Mistletoe at the entrance to Lydney hillfort

Downs over 20 miles distant (**57**) and the bluestones from Mynydd Preseli 120 miles away (**48, 49**). Ores of copper, tin and gold were from the west and north or came from outside of the British Isles. Cornish tin was exploited for tin bronze from the beginning of the second millennium BC. Lead, often occurring with copper, was being mined in the Mendips by at least Roman times and perhaps earlier (**p. 73**). Locations of iron ore extraction, although mainly in the south-east, were more generally distributed, and in western Britain there was wide use of bog ores.

Early extraction in any one area may have been where sources were obvious, as in coastal cliffs, but which we do not know about because they are now worked out or destroyed. Visibility was enhanced where high concentrations of metal ores near the surface inhibited tree-growth, although blanket peat, quite extensive by the second millennium BC, could have obscured some outcrops. Later sources may have been identified by more directed prospecting and thus be distant from settlements and in areas more difficult of access. With regard to materials, purity and ease of extraction of concentrated materials like high-grade ores were relevant early on; later sources were often related to changing extraction technologies, as with the shift from oxidised to sulphide ores of copper.

Selection, or rejection, of particular sites may have been constrained by land tenure.

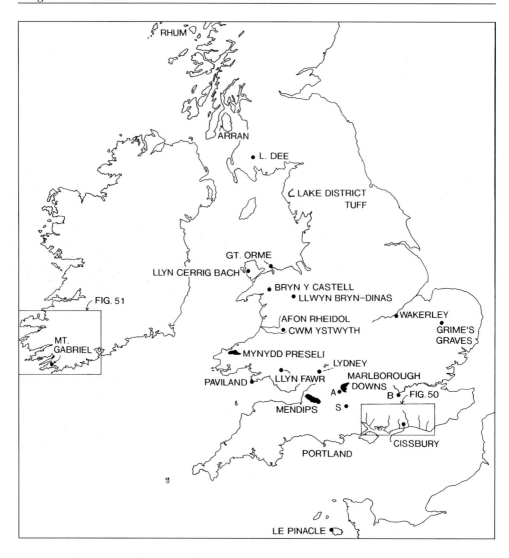

47   *Sites mentioned in chap. 5. A, Avebury; B, Brookland; S, Stonehenge*

There may also have been an association with other, contemporaneous, activities which were precedential and which took place only at particular times of the year, like seasonal herding or occasional gatherings of whole communities. This may have been the case with the flint-mines of early farming communities, and it is probably significant that these, like the causewayed camps, were often sited in deep woodland. In the South Downs in Sussex, there is a complementary distribution of flint-mines, causewayed camps and long barrows of the fourth and third millennia BC, which suggests an equivalence of meaning at least at one level (**50**).

Some sites may have been selected for their difficulty of access as with the axe factories in the English Lake District or for spectacular natural rock formations like Le Pinacle on the north-west coast of Jersey, in both cases so as to imbue extraction with mystique

48   Carn Meini, Mynydd Preseli, mid-summer sunset

and power. In some cases rocks may have been deliberately placed to enhance meaning, as at Carn Meini in the Preseli Hills **(49)**. The relative inaccessibility of the Mt Gabriel copper mines could mean an industry in decline, but the location may also have been magical. So extraction was not neutral, related solely to the production of an end product in terms of technological or maximising criteria. It was a medium through which people could express and establish relationships. We saw this with butchery **(p. 14)**, and it should be familiar ground by now. In this way, specific materials were used not only for their technical properties but also for their visual or magical ones and the historical links of the site. Today, for example, Welsh gold from Rhayader is often used for rings because of its association with royalty. The relationship is between the person who gets the ring, their perceptions of royalty and the meaning these have for that person themselves and other people. It is not to do immediately with any physical properties of Rhayader or the Rhayader gold, although it may have been originally.

So the land of mining, quarrying and collecting was a land that was embedded in meanings. It had a significance in terms of visuality and other activities and it was a medium of expression. It may not have been very much about the extraction of inorganic raw materials at all.

Impact

The effects of mining and quarrying on the environment need to be considered at different scales. Locally there were the mine-shafts, quarries and tips which, although not extensive were, because of their intensiveness, often highly durable. This is seen with the flint-mines of prehistoric farmers as at Grimes Graves near Thetford in the

49   The highest point of Carn Meini, Mynydd Preseli

East Anglian Breckland and some of the Sussex sites which were clearings in woodland and are still significant landscape features. More widely there was the use of charcoal, peat and wood for fuel in fire-setting the rock, and this may have made huge inroads on the vegetation. There was use of bone, antler, wood and stone for tools. Different stone types for use as mauls in the quarrying of Gt Langdale rhyolite indicate exploitation by people from at least two different areas of the Lake District. There were constructions associated with supplying water to mines like the aqueduct and leats to the Roman gold mine at Dolaucothi and for drainage like the Copa Hill launder **(p. 72)**. There may have been specific settlements for mine and quarry-workers, or the processes may have been integrated into the farming cycle, as with the summer tending of cattle in uplands. Seasonal, and especially summer, exploitation of mines and quarries may also have been encouraged because of the demands of the local subsistence economy and the problems of mining in bad weather.

There were several prehistoric copper mines in the British Isles. The group on the Mizen and Beara Peninsulas, Co. Cork, includes Mt Gabriel **(51)**, where mining took place between 1700 and 1500 BC. The location is stunning, going up to over 1000ft and overlooking Roaringwater Bay. Activity was extensive, with 31 shafts, mostly in an area about 1000 x 250yds. It was also intensive. No shaft was longer than 40ft, although some, unexcavated, may be up to 100ft judging by the size of their spoil tips. Wood species from the mines were oak, hazel, ash, willow and pine, and there was an alder shovel, so there was quite a diversity of local trees. Each shaft had an associated dump where primary breakdown of the rock and selection of visibly mineralised fragments took place. The ores were mainly carbonates (malachite) and oxides with some low-grade sulphide. Breakdown, probably fire-aided, was by means of sandstone cobbles of 1-2kg brought from the coast in their thousands and selected for their hardness and resilience. The actual settlements where the miners lived, however, are unknown. Distribution of the

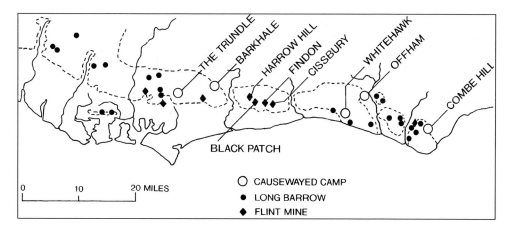

50   *The Sussex chalk (dashed line) with sites of the fourth millennium BC. (Based on Russell 1997)*

Mt Gabriel ores may have been quite widespread because there is no metal assemblage of the relevant age and metallurgical composition in the area, although there is a general association with type Ballyvalley bronze axes (**51**). Mining and distribution of ores may have been associated with new controlling elites in the area, intensification of agriculture and innovations in burial and ceremony. Links through regional exchange networks with tin supplies from Cornwall or Brittany would have been vital. There were probably earlier copper mines in the general area, judging by the metal composition of earlier artefacts.

The Great Orme above Llandudno, on a headland of Carboniferous Limestone on the North Wales coast, is another magnificent setting for prehistoric copper mines. The area, at 460-540ft OD, is naturally defended by steep slopes and cliffs except for the Pyllau Valley, and this is overlooked by an earthwork enclosure, Pen-y-Dinas. The headland was probably open vegetation in the second millennium BC because of exposure to sea spray and wind and perhaps because of high copper levels in the soil. It would have provided a focus for grazing animals and ritual activity, and it would be surprising if it had not been visited by people well before the mining. Earthworks of the causewayed-camp sort may yet be found and indeed there is no reason why those of Pen-y-Dinas could not be fourth millennium even if the numerous huts within it are later.

The green copper ores would have been strikingly visible at the surface. Exploitation in the second millennium BC was on a large-scale, covering more than 260,000sq ft, and took place between c1700-1000 BC. Opencast areas, at least 115 x 65ft in extent and 23ft deep, are seen as the initial workings. Underground passages, of which there are over 3 miles, go to 230ft below the surface. Almost 1.5 million cubic feet (40,000 cubic metres) of material was removed. Then there is evidence of re-working, after two or three centuries (later second millennium BC), specifically for previously ignored sulphide ores. These are harder and more difficult to extract than the carbonates, and fire-setting and metal tools, for both of which there is evidence, may have been used specifically in this. We know nothing about where the timber came from for these endeavours, or where the settlements were that were associated with them; they were presumably in valleys,

71

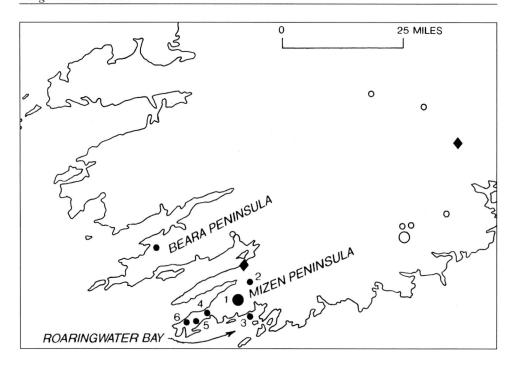

51 *Prehistoric copper metallurgy in south-west Ireland. Black circles = mines: 1, Mt Gabriel; 2, Derrycarhoon; 3, Horse Island; 4, Ballyrisode; 5, Boulysallagh; 6, Callaros Oughter. Small open circles = Ballyvalley axes; large open circle = the Bandon axe hoard; diamonds = stone moulds. (Based on O'Brien 1990)*

perhaps close to the sea where Llandudno is now. Like other prehistoric copper mines in the British Isles, there is no trace of smelting, such as slag or hearths, on the Great Orme.

As well as the clear and intensive local effects of mining, wider influences, such as the liberation of toxic metals into the atmosphere and soil-water, the disruption of land-surfaces, the deposition of waste materials and the alteration of vegetation can be identified in sediments and soils.

There is a group of copper mining areas in west Wales, 12.5 miles inland of Aberystwyth. One of these, Copa Hill, is in a remote location along the north side of Cwmystwyth, and at 1378ft it is well above the limit of historical enclosure. Pollen analysis of adjacent peats 355yds to the north on the plateau at 1640ft OD indicates woodland of hazel, oak, alder and birch, in descending order of abundance, that was quite open at the time of mining. There was also evidence linking human activity with blanket peat formation, beginning in the early centuries of the second millennium BC, and both this and the openness of the woodland are thought to have been related to pastoralism rather than to the mining activities specifically. C-14 dates for the mining itself span 2365-900 BC, although mining may not have been continuous. The earliest date is from the charred end of an alder launder found within the mine and with metal axe-marks on it; this may have been to carry water out of the mine. There was removal of trees during the period of mining, but this was only small-scale perhaps owing to the low intensity of the mining. Woodland management is suggested by the selective removal of hazel and oak in steps, each followed by a slight recovery. A layer of small charcoal contemporary with later mining may have been from fire-setting; this also coincided with an increase of heather. There was much grassland and possibly cereal cultivation, so there was farming going on as well. It was all quite diverse: open woodland and grassland around the mines, the mines themselves, some heather, and the beginnings of blanket peat growth on the plateau, perhaps *via* grassland and *Rumex* vegetation as on Dartmoor **(p. 28)**. For a short period at the end of mining, trees returned to their previous densities. Ultimately there was a general decrease in grassland and trees and an increase in heather which was sustained, with hiccups, to the present-day.

Iron from podsolized and peaty soils may have been the source of metalworking in the Welsh Marches and North Wales. Vegetation history at Bryn y Castell hillfort in Snowdonia at 1246ft OD **(52)**, where iron-smelting and bloom-smithing went on from the later first millennium to the early Roman period **(p. 77)** was investigated from a valley bog and blanket peat. Like the work at Copa Hill, the Bryn y Castell investigation was designed to test the hypothesis that metalworking had a significant impact on the local woodland. But things are deeper than this, and concerns range from the integration of other activities with metalworking to the place of metalworking in the history of the area — why it was taking place there and what influence it had on future history.

Thus woodland was thinning out c1000 yrs before iron-working began, and by the time it did so, the area was largely open, with grassland, areas of sorrels (*Rumex* spp.) and ribwort plantain (*Plantago lanceolata*) **(72)**, possibly some cereal cultivation, a valley bog and blanket peat. There was still some local woodland, the largest area of which was closest to the hillfort **(52**, site A) and mainly of alder. Ironworking had only a localised impact on this, with small-scale removal of some tree species, especially birch and alder, but also oak and hazel. Ironworking phases occurred from 70 BC-50 AD and from AD 150-250. These were implicated in the vegetational history up to c250 yds around the site (BYC-H and BYC), but not further away (BYC-3 and -4), and in periods of burning as shown by layers of fine charcoal. It is an elegant piece of research. Interestingly there was no response from the usual plant indicators of burning like cow-wheat (*Melampyrum*), bracken (*Pteridium*) and crowberry (*Empetrum*), so the charcoal is likely derived from the metalworking itself. A Roman road within 330ft of the site, built in the late AD 70s, adds further diversity, especially as the borders may have been kept clear of woodland to prevent ambush. Subsequently, woodland recovered to its previous levels except in the immediate vicinity of the hillfort.

Heavy-metal analysis of alluvium and peat in the valley of the River Lox Yeo of the western Mendip Hills **(47)**, has identified periods of inwash of lead and zinc. The first of these was in the fourth millennium BC, presumably from erosion of the metalliferous limestone soils as a result of agriculture. Mining itself is first signalled in the first half of the first millennium BC. During the Roman period it is seen archaeologically as shafts and tips, and at Winscombe in the upper reaches of the Lox Yeo it is also registered in the alluvium, although atmospheric pollution from smelting at the Roman settlement of Charterhouse, 7 miles to the east, is a possible source for this as well. Mining in the seventeenth-nineteenth centuries AD is also matched in the alluvium, and the most recent

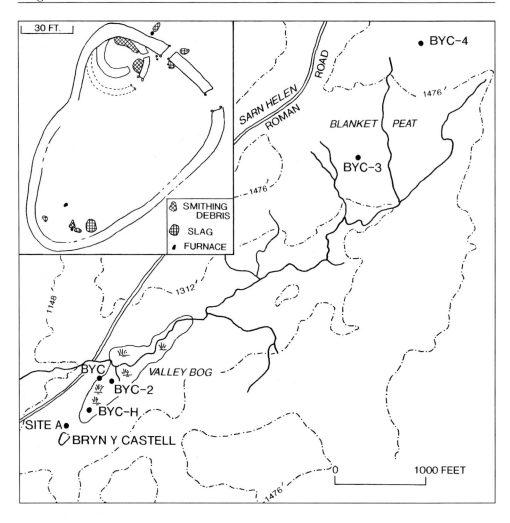

52   *Bryn y Castell; location of pollen sites and iron-working remains. (Based on Crew 1986; Mighall & Chambers 1997)*

phase of this saw the re-working of older slags and spoil. High lead values in the surface layers are mainly from car emissions.

The direct effects of the metal-mining sediments themselves, especially on valley environments and river channel dynamics, can also be examined. During the historical period in mid-Wales, increases in river sediment load affected flow, nutrient properties and deposition in areas where overbank-flooding took place. There was also the deposition of large quantities of mining waste which did not get into the rivers but which altered their course. This was substantial where the valleys were narrow and steep-sided, as in Cwm Ystwyth and Cwm Rheidol where there are extensive widths of bare stony floor. Toxicity of the dumped materials, coming from crushing mills, dressing floors, flotation plants and spoil, was also a factor, killing the vegetation and causing soil erosion. Lead, zinc, copper and cadmium were present, and where the dumps persisted they were a problem for many years. Although this study relates to historic-age mining the effects are likely to have been felt from as early as the beginning of the second millennium BC, while stream erosion of exposed lodes probably contributed metals to alluvial sediments throughout the entire period since the Ice Age.

Another sedimentary record of heavy-metal deposition is from Loch Dee in Galloway, although here the origin was atmospheric, unlike the situation in the Lox Yeo and Afon Ystwyth where it was largely subaerial. There was an increase of lead and copper deposition within the catchment as early as AD 1400, probably due to local mining and smelting. This is a century or so earlier than at other sites, and much earlier than the first documentation of lead mining and smelting in Galloway at AD 1650. Later increases of lead and zinc, c1840, correlate with the start of mass coal use.

Human bones provide another medium for the deposition of metal compounds. Lead, for example, was accreted during life, as in bones from Roman York, and levels were unaffected by the burial environment. Analysis could provide an index of drinking-water contamination in mining areas. Correlation with levels in sediments of the same age could suggest one of the ways in which this particular cation and water moved from the biophysical environment to the human body. But lead also gets into drink and food from the pipes and tanks of water systems and the linings of cooking pots, and there may even have been deliberate poisoning. So the situation is complex.

Society itself is also a medium for the deposition of signals of metal-working, as seen in current perceptions of lead as an environmental poison and in the manipulation of these perceptions in commerce and industry. In academic circles, the use of ancient copper mines has continued to the present-day in the debate over their age. A post-medieval date for certain copper mines, based on the supposition that the C-14 dates are from peat and bog-wood fuel which was prehistoric, can no longer be sustained. But the debate is more about the foolishness of accepting ideas solely because they are attractive, rather than about the age of the copper mines. In South Wales, the consequences of closing almost all the coal mines in the last two decades, like the acute problems of unemployment, the landscaping of the workings and the conversion of some to educational sites, have provided classic examples of social and political expression, much of which has nothing to do with the welfare of the former mining communities or the landscapes at all.

Abandonment

Which brings us to abandonment. Mines, quarries and other areas of raw material collection have varied histories, often seeing several episodes of abandonment and re-use, especially where there were changing technologies of extraction. The term 'abandonment', however, must be used carefully because it can have different meanings. Usually it means the abandonment of particular activities or of a site by a specific group of people. But no area or site is ever totally abandoned. Just as we can refer to the abandonment of La Cotte de St Brelade for mammoth killing and butchery but see its continuing use for the specialised extraction of sinew and still later use for squatter settlement, so we can see inorganic raw material extraction sites as having had a sequence of uses different in intensity and kind and probably by different groups of people. An area of woodland

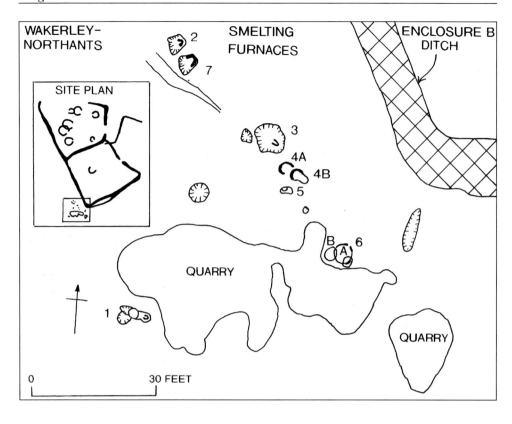

53   *Wakerley; iron-smelting furnaces. (Based on Jackson & Ambrose 1978)*

cleared for mining could later be used for settlement, or disused mines could be taken over for hiding stolen animals or smuggled goods. And the meaning of a place which has been created by particular activities is seldom lost. The Great Orme could have seen the start of mining not just because of the ore but through its historical or phenomenological associations, so the end of mining sees a continuation or even an enhancement of these, which thus carries on and is quite the opposite of abandonment. Mining, quarrying and collecting inorganic raw materials have to be seen in a continuum of meaning not just as something which started and ended *in vacuo*.

Metal- and stone-working

The working of inorganic raw materials was not just about making tools with a specific end artefact and function in sight. Nor was it just about style or the technological limitations of particular raw materials. It was also about relations between people while the artefacts were being made and how people expressed themselves through their work. It was the same for an axe factory, an exchange network or a stone axe. Extraction, metal- and stone-working and the manufacture of artefacts each played as much a role as the use of the artefacts themselves in the establishment of localities, and each stage and the

54   Dolmen de Couperon, allée couverte, Jersey, showing the semi-porthole

artefacts were modified accordingly. To quote M-A Dobres: 'Technology concerns *artifice* as much as it concerns artefacts'. There really is no such thing as a finished artefact.

Objects and people interface in big life schemes of metaphor and symbolism; they do so, too, at an intermediate scale of communication in areas and regions; and there are the intimacies of person-to-person transactions as localities.

Richard Hingley has looked at big life schemes in iron-working in later prehistory and the Roman period. The connection between agriculture and metalworking was close from the start with the collecting of ore from fields **(p. 66)**. Then '. . . like crops, it was cleaned, winnowed and ground . . . , with smelting (baking) in a furnace (oven) to produce a bloom (loaf) continuing the domestic metaphor'. The location of metal-working areas was often in settlements, although sometimes just outside them, and often in specific areas. At Wakerley, Northants, iron-working took place over much of the settlement, but there were specific places for it. Some smelting furnaces, consisting of fired-clay-lined pits, were in corners of the settlement; there was a group of seven in an area just outside the corner of one of the enclosures **(53)**; and there were others also outside the settlement some distance away. Smithing, too, often occurred in a domestic context, using domestic hearths. At a house at Brooklands, Weybridge, Surrey, smelting and smithing both went on but in separate areas, the smelting to the south-west of the house, the smithing to the south-east. Smithing can also be more specialised in its locations and restricted to smithies which were, again, sometimes at settlement edges. At Bryn y Castell **(52)** **(p. 73)**, iron-smelting furnaces occurred in three areas of the enclosure and smithing in others. Locations close to settlement entrances, as with middens **(p. 57)**, symbolised status, and their precise positioning may have had cosmological meanings, as in relation to the sun,

55   *Sarsen polissoir on Totterdown, north Wiltshire*

as well as practical ones, as in relation to wind direction. Combinations of low status, like uncleanliness, and high status, like mystique, may also have been involved. The positioning of these activities and people, including noises, smells, smoke and flames, established a fine detail of localities. Associated ritual, especially symbolising procreation, might be expected with the transformations from stone to metal and smithing. Thus metalworking required considerable fuel at almost all its stages, and this means charcoal or wood and clearing or managing woodland for them **(p. 73)**. The plants that grew up in the cleared areas may themselves have been significant in the regeneration symbolism, like rosebay willowherb or fireweed (*Epilobium angustifolium*) was for Londoners after the last war, and have been used in associated rituals.

The language of writing about symbolism and metaphor is stylistic. For example: '. . . there is an irreducible core that ties the technology to the closest analogue in human experience — the drama of procreation . . . Over this are layer upon layer of culturally specific symbols that not only articulate the process but are believed to act homeopathically to make it happen'. (E.W. Herbert, cited in Hingley 1997.) But it needs to be shown how these metaphors work at the scale of individuals in everyday life.

Thus much of tool use is about communication, especially in crossing boundaries, which people did (and we do) all the time. With small metal and stone artefacts, their size allowed mobility and an even more complex history of meanings than a fixed setting. The products of extraction and manufacture were circulated, used, often re-used

56   Close-up of the Totterdown polissoir. The dished area was for smoothing stone axe blades and the linear areas were for straightening the blades and removing deformities

and deposited. Rubbing was common, with meaning being about movement across boundaries, access and expression. Thus the bevelled pebbles of the Obanians **(p. 46)** may have been more about smoothness *per se* than grinding lyme grass seeds. An end stone in the Dolmen de Couperon on Jersey **(54)** has a hole in it which has been rubbed, and the location of this site is probably significant in that it overlooks a steep valley running down to the sea which would have provided an ideal trap for game. Stone axeheads of the third millennium BC were polished, perhaps to permeate them with specific socialities. The sites of polishing and sharpening, on either portable stones or immobile rock, then became equally significant. The polishers, or *polissoirs* as they are called with reference to the sarsen ones in Wessex, are in edge contexts. They can signify changes from life to death as when they occur in tombs like the West Kennet long barrow near Avebury; from public to private as with stones of the nearby West Kennet Avenue; or arable to pasture as at the edges of cultivated areas **(55, 56)**. They occur on the borders from domestic to wild areas as in areas of wasteland and poor soils, and which may have been meeting places like causewayed camps but without their formal boundaries **(57)**. We can also note Alasdair Whittle's observations concerning the pairs of rough (undressed) and smooth (dressed) stones in the Stonehenge trilithons.

Destruction of land with mining debris or heavy-metal pollution needed watching. Concepts of keeping and owning emerged; restitution may have become relevant. Places became part of material culture and could have been exchanged between people. They were also enhanced in meaning with the deposition of metalwork, and this took place in graves and hoards, often under boundary banks. It also occurred, especially from the later second and earlier first millennia BC (1600-1350 BC) onwards, in bogs and lakes **(58)** as

57   *Totterdown (above) and Overton Down, Wiltshire, showing areas of clay, sarsen stones and hawthorn bushes*

at Llyn Fawr, Glamorgan, and Llyn Cerrig Bach, Anglesey, and in rivers like the Thames. Many of the objects in hoards are associated with birth and killing, like ploughs, butchery knives, sickles and axes; and these concepts are seen, too, in scrap as currency bars in the form of spits, ploughshares and swords. Hoards were often about the perpetuation of community boundaries, especially when they were weakening, as we saw earlier with other forms of deposition in Orkney just as sites were about to be abandoned **(p. 53)**.

This too applied to mines, where perpetuation of their significance was marked with ritual depositions when they became disused. Thus the Copa Hill launder was put into the mine vertically and at Grimes Graves they buried a dog.

Not objects and sites, nor people and animals may have been so important. There were structures to be sure but these were of myths and legends, kinship and other community interplays, and the every-day relationships of the expressive order as played out in

58 *A watery hollow in a wooded area, evoking the pools in which metalwork was deposited in the second and first millennia BC*

localities. There was a network of places, or locales, like the *polissoirs*, the causewayed camps and the mines which were physically fixed but whose meaning changed as they were constituted variously as localities. There was a network of small artefacts which were moved around and used as props by people in the establishments of localities. And there was a network of community relationships which was partly constituted in kinship and residence and partly in where people were. Where these networks interacted, further localities were created which survived for a while and were then dispersed as the people went on or changed their ideas. Archaeologists often make the distinction between 'sites', where there is a concentration and diversity of activity where things happen and are repeated, and 'offsites' which were the areas in between. Equally, this distinction is just as often dismantled in an attempt to view the entire land as significant in people's lives. In fact we could reverse the whole business and say that sites are where there is such familiarity that meetings and interactions become mundane — like going to the bread shop, to the butchers or to Mass — and that it is the occasional meetings in offsite areas like with your Aunt in the street once a year or with a stranger in the park that are of much more significance and durability in lives.

That is certainly how it is for me.

6 The Cheviot Hills and the Milfield Basin

The Cheviot Hills start about 20 miles north of Hadrian's Wall (**73**). They rise to 2674ft and their north-east/south-west watershed is part of the border between Scotland and the south. They contrast with the valleys of the Rivers Teviot and Tweed to the north-west and north (**59**) and especially with the Milfield Basin to the north-east which is the southern part of the Tweed lowlands and for which the hills provide a stunning backdrop like a wall (**64**). Most of Northumberland's rivers, including the North Tyne, rise in the Cheviots, usually in deep and narrow valleys with many branches and secret areas hidden by turns and spurs winding up into the hills (**60**). And the same is so on the north side into Scotland. Because of these features, there are only small areas on the valley floors suitable for arable, but the valley sides and some areas of the plateaus have been widely cultivated in the past as can be seen by terraces and ridge-and-furrow (**61, 65, 66**). There are no roads through the main massif but by walking it is very easy to slip across the watersheds from one valley to another and into completely different lands. To the north is the rich lowland farming area of the Merse, punctuated to the north-west by the volcanic core of the Eildon Hills which seem to be visible from everywhere (**77**). And then there are the Lammermuir Hills. In the south-west are the springs of Liddel Water and the beginnings of Liddesdale which runs for over 20 miles to join the River Esk, shortly before entering the Solway Firth a few miles north of Carlisle.

Richard Tipping has studied the land and vegetation of the Cheviots for the sixth to third millennia BC, mainly by pollen analysis and C-14, and it is on his work that the following account is based. There are rare and scattered finds of stone axe-heads on high inter-fluves in the central Cheviots and more numerous finds lower down, below c500 to 650ft OD (**59**). Likewise there are few long cairns in the main Cheviot massif, most being around the periphery of the hills, and pottery of the period shows an even more lowland distribution. This kind of archaeological barrenness we will meet again in first millennium BC Cumbria, where it is seen as reflecting variously a cultural backwater, a lack of preservation of insubstantial timber or turf structures, or an absence of discovery **(p. 107)**. It was Tipping's aim to investigate these kinds of possibilities, but here for a much earlier time. Three sites provide the central data (**59**). They are lake deposits from Yetholm Loch in a confined lowland basin at 330ft OD (**62**), a peat bog at Sourhope at 974ft and another at Swindon Hill at 1204ft OD both deep within the hills of the upper Bowmont Valley (**60**).

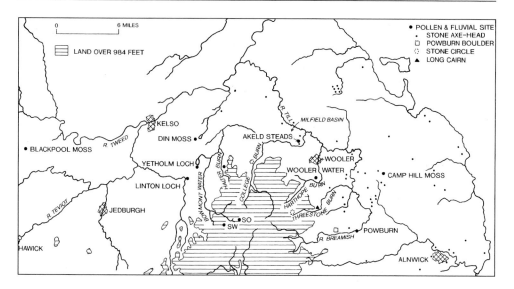

59   *The Cheviots showing sites mentioned in chap. 6. (Based on Tipping 1996; Topping 1997)*

The early centuries

The main tree throughout was alder. Around Yetholm Loch there was also oak, elm and hazel while in the upper Bowmont Valley there was predominantly hazel and birch, with some oak but no elm. This woodland may have gone right over the summit ridges. The differences between the two areas may be due to poorer soils in the Bowmont Valley rather than altitude, although a combination of factors is likely. At Sourhope, from c4625 BC, there was opening of the dry woods around the bog and the carr woods on it, with evidence for pasture (*Plantago* and *Rumex*), suggesting clearance by grazing, and fire (*Melampyrum*). This was followed by partial regeneration of birch and oak after 4050 BC. A more tenuous woodland disturbance took place around Yetholm Loch at c4600 BC. These episodes may reflect hunter-gatherer activity or just animals creating open areas through their grazing, browsing and other activities **(p. 26)**. There are not the numerous rock outcrops in the Cheviots that we find on Dartmoor and Carn Meini and which might have provided a focus for some of these activities, although there are some. Instead, the foci of openings may have been around springs, as Ian Simmons has shown with his work in the North York Moors, and in areas of dying trees caused by peat growth on the hills and by beavers along the rivers. There also seems to have been little influence of fire in the Cheviots in these later centuries of the fifth millennium, with two of the common consequences of this, namely soil erosion and acid heathland, being quite insignificant.

Woodland use and sacred lands

Later activity — its nature and, especially, its location — may have been related to these early openings in the woods. At Yetholm Loch c3825-3540 BC elm pollen fell from 8% to

60   *Cocklawfoot in the Cheviot Hills part way up the Bowmont Valley*

<1% and at Din Moss, 2.5 miles away, there was a similar fall but 300-500 years earlier, c4452/4035-4340/3985 BC. This could have been caused by people lopping off elm leaves and thin branches for fodder for cattle which apparently they like rather than other species of tree such as oak. The branches could have been cut off with axes of stone or just ripped off and this might have weakened the trees' resistance to disease from fungi; an endemic disease could have become epidemic. People might also have been lopping the fruits off for the same purpose in the late winter, when they are especially prominent (**63**), and this would have had a particularly strong impact on future pollen output in that it targetted the flowering shoots. Cattle also rip the bark off elm trees by pulling it up as whole strips, a trick they may have learnt by doing the same with ivy only more easily, and this too could have affected pollen production. A shift to wetter or cooler conditions (**p. 95**) could also have enhanced or triggered a reduction in flowering, especially if the elm were close to its northern or altitudinal limit here as is suggested by its absence from the Bowmont Valley. However, Bolton Fell Moss where the work on wetness phases was done is 42 miles away and to the south-west, so conditions there might have been a lot wetter anyway. Several factors could have been operating together to retard or speed up the effect of a single one which ultimately caused the fall in elm pollen production, and the absence of synchroneity between its occurrence at Din Moss and Yetholm Loch does not mean that a single factor at a single time was not operating.

People could have been using woodlands in various ways for a protracted period in the fifth and fourth millennia BC in keeping cattle in them. In the winter they would have moved with their cattle to grasslands in river valleys, the uplands or at the coast, or used elm fodder which had been earlier cut and stored from the woodlands. Microwear anlysis of cattle teeth could tell us a lot about the whereabouts of winter feeding grounds or what sort of fodder was being used. Drying and storage of elm leaves and branches

61   Terraces in the Bowmont Valley

could have been done in enclosures or storehouses away from dampness and animals, and occasionally we do find evidence for rectangular stone or timber structures which could have been for this; hearths at soil level may have been for heating and drying overhead storage areas. Or the animals could have been penned. Another possibility would be to ring-bark trees in the early summer and lop the branches and leaves off during the winter as and when required, thus solving the drying and storing problems in one go and at the same time allowing coppice to spring up from the trunk below the ring-barking, providing further fodder. Particular areas of woodland would have been managed at one time and then people would have moved on. At Yetholm Loch this sort of wholesale damage is likely because there was some soil in-wash into the loch after the first fall in elm pollen as early as 3550 BC, perhaps where there was also cattle trampling around the waters' edge. The absence of other effects in these pollen diagrams, except for a slight appearance of lime and ash which might have been moving into the areas where the elms had ultimately died, supports this model.

Although there has been a lot of discussion of the cause of this fall in elm pollen, in some ways the cause is not so important as the ecological effects. *Something was going on.* Whether it was just a decrease in flowering intensity, or the lopping of branches and fruits, or the death of entire trees, it would have been integrated into people's lives. There was probably a lot of dead wood and then dead trees, and if they were in stands openings would have developed allowing light-loving herbs to move in. These were like other openings in woodland around tors, monadnocks and areas of blanket-peat **(p. 28)**, and they provided foci for settlement, planting crops and keeping animals. If small, as is likely, they may not have been registered in the pollen record because of the surrounding trees keeping the pollen of herbs in, unless the pollen catchment was close to the opening. But as they got bigger they were, and this is just what occurred at Yetholm Loch some 300

62   Yetholm Loch

years after the start of the fall in elm pollen. There was the beginnings of a decline in other trees, an increase in grasses and the first appearance of ribwort plantain (*Plantago lanceolata*) (**72**). Probable cereal pollen first appears at Yetholm Loch c2600 BC.

At Sourhope there was early fourth millennium woodland clearance and pastoral use of the land. After a break, this became more substantial c2850 BC, with some cereal cultivation, and lasted for about 200 years. Woodland then closed over once more. At Swindon Hill, the record did not start until c3450 BC when peat growth started, probably in dense carr woodland of alder and birch. There was grassland with *Rumex* at the start of the sequence but no plantain. Woodland disturbance and cereal cultivation took place from 2850 BC and the pollen was sufficiently well preserved to indicate barley and wheat. This continued for many centuries.

Thus there was considerable woodland use, woodland clearance, pasture and cultivation in the upper Bowmont Valley of the Cheviots and out onto the lower-lying areas around Yetholm Loch to the north. Although we might say that this is in contrast to the paucity of more conventional archaeological data, this should be viewed positively in that the absence of such data is actually an indication that kinds of management were taking place that did not require enclosures, substantial structures of stone or turf, or ceremonial monuments. Peter Topping sees these early inhabitants of the Cheviots '. . . as forest farmers, opportunists who *had to* take advantage of whatever could be won from within the gaps in the forest canopy . . .', with mobility 'partly stimulated by soil degeneration . . . *forcing* groups to traverse the landscape in search of more productive locations' (my italics). It is, however, difficult to judge cultural complexity or depth from any of these data. Woodland life should not be undervalued. There may have been a closeness with the environment which was neither determinist nor marginal. Furthermore, it is perhaps

63   *Elm* (Ulmus sp.) *fruits in late winter showing their distinctiveness against the opening leaves*

too structured to see a distinct contrast between low intensity use in the upper Bowmont Valley and more substantial farming in the area around Yetholm Loch; or to see a shift of activity from *simple* forms of pastoralism in upland woodland to more complex agricultural life in the lowlands, especially as a response to soil deterioration; and too regionalistic to extend this sort of pattern to other valleys and other headwater areas generally. In these kinds of models which are both progress-oriented and micro-regionalised one tends to underestimate the diversity of settlement and subsistence strategies engendered by the playing out of interactions within individual communities. In fact it is easier to explain the absence of monuments in a relatively mobile woodland husbandry rather than in open country where they would have been more relevant. The long period of woodland life and the precise knowledge of the land it had engendered made any such embellishments superfluous. The land was structured within the people's minds.

  And there were, in fact, some monuments, and they were intimately structured in relation to natural features. Stone circles and a henge were located at stream confluences and were probably in small clearings, the stones and banks mimicking the crags and slopes of the steep-sided valleys and natural amphitheatres in which they lay. The circle at Hethpool is on a broad terrace at the mouth of the College Valley surrounded by steep slopes. At Threestoneburn, the stone circle is at a stream confluence at the head of a valley which descends past Dod Hill and a small long cairn; walking up valley to it you have the massive bulk of the Cheviot on the horizon (**60**). A cup-marked boulder in the valley at Powburn is similarly located with reference to light, land, water and springs. These monuments may have been located, too, for their views at particular celestial events and they may also have been route markers from lowland to upland and across the Cheviot Hills.

64   The wall of the Cheviots across the Milfield Basin

The Milfield Basin

In the Milfield Basin, an area of prime agricultural land to the immediate east of the Cheviots (**59, 64**), there is a different signal. Here, on gravel terrace surfaces of the River Till, monuments are numerous, albeit ploughed out except for two standing stones. There are ceremonial enclosures, numerous henges, an avenue which resembles a cursus but is more irregular than usual for this type of monument, and alignments of pits, in an area of a few square miles and generally reminiscent of the complexes in the Welland Valley (**p. 40**). And as in the Welland Valley and the Cheviots there was analogue structuring of monuments and natural features. Henges, especially, were oriented with the axis through their centres and entrances aligned with adjacent water courses, as if incorporating the life-giving powers of rivers and streams in an architectural symbolling. There was overbank river sedimentation at Akeld Steads (3400-2650 BC) on the edge of the Milfield Basin so there may have been greater use of these areas than the high Cheviots for agriculture. The orientation of the henges may then be seen as reflecting a dialectic of fear and thanksgiving, fear from the erosion of valuable arable land, thanksgiving for its upgrading by the fertile waters of the floods. Intriguingly, pollen analysis suggests some woodland regeneration at this time. But this need not be at odds with overbank flooding nor with continued human activity; there may well have been a revertence to woodland husbandry. Perhaps woodland, too, explains the irregularity of the avenue, as we suggested earlier for parts of the Eylesbarrow reeve on Dartmoor (**p. 29**).

Later histories

Survey by Historic Scotland of the upper Bowmont Water Valley has provided the archaeological focus for later settlement studies and detailed palynology of the third and second millennia BC. For these, there is more conventional archaeological evidence for settlement in the Cheviots (**65, 66, 67**), substantial pollen evidence for clearance and land-use, and substantial soil erosion as seen in the river valleys. Clearances took place at Swindon Hill from c2350 BC, at Sourhope c2250 BC and at Yetholm Loch slightly later, with contemporaneous fluvial aggradations at the Wooler Water and Halter Burn indicating upland erosion in two other northern valleys. Field archaeology suggests a change in the nature of upland settlement during this period towards intensive clearance and arable agriculture, lasting until c1250 BC.

65   *The Castles fort, Cheviots, showing the multiple banks at one of the entrances*

66   *The Shearers stone row from the fort of Hownam Rings. The stone row goes across a col from one valley to another and beyond there are two banks*

67   *One of the Shearers, showing the puddling caused by sheep and which provides drinking water for animals*

In the first millennium there was the establishment of large numbers of palisaded settlements, forts and other kinds of embanked enclosures (**65**) in the uplands of the Cheviots. At Hownam Rings there are linear banks and ditches in the area of the fort which may have been built before the fort when the area was enclosed for agriculture or pasture. There is also a line of stones widely spaced called 'The Shearers' which goes from one side of the ridge where the hillfort is to the other, across a col in effect, and there are cultivation ridges between the stones and one of the linear banks (**66, 67**). Other forts, like Park Law above Sourhope, also have associated linear earthworks and in some cases they seem to be focussed in a radial fashion on the summits where the forts are sited. Some of the forts are quite small and yet they can have up to four or even five ramparts and quite complex entrances where the ends of the ramparts form an arc so that you do not get a straight view in or out. Numerous houses within the forts show that these were settlements that were lived in for at least a part of the year. Winters were probably inhospitable, to say the least, and the settlements may have been deserted then. Many of the forts, of which there are considerable numbers in the Cheviots, are sited on prominent hills separated by a col from the main upland area; or they are or on spurs at the ends of ridges above the confluence of two streams, as with the Dewerstone (**p. 28**). In some places, several forts are inter-visible. So there were many locales, some small and intricate as around the entrances and adjacent houses, others larger like the distribution of linear earthworks, cultivated land and pasture, and some extending over wide areas like the relationships of the forts to the topography and other forts. But many of these sites had a long history, like Hownam Rings, with the embankments and huts, for example, being in and out of use and their number varying; so the nature of the locales and the potential for different kinds of relationship as localities varied. We saw this, too, at Edin's Hall (**43**).

There was cultivation of the uplands in association with these prehistoric settlements. Narrow- or cord-rig sometimes underlies them, sometimes runs up to them, and can also

68   The River Breamish near Powburn showing colluvium in the river bank

overlie them partially or totally (**66**). This form of cultivation is quite extensive, going up to 1377ft OD in Northumberland and down to almost sea-level as beneath the Roman fort at Wallsend and adjacent to Hadrian's Wall at Tarraby Lane, Carlisle. It may have been in use for several centuries so it cannot be tied to a narrow period or settlement type. Some of the narrower and more irregular valley-side cultivation terraces may belong to this period also, although the more substantial of these probably belong to the historical periods. Soil erosion took place in the closing two centuries of the first millennium BC, as seen at Yetholm Loch in an inwash of clay and in the valleys of the Breamish and Bowmont where gravels grade up into agricultural colluvium (**68**).

The adjacency of the northern and eastern valleys of the Cheviot Hills and the lowland of the Milfield basin and the River Till provides a series of locales as intricate as anywhere in the British Isles. In a relatively small area there are lakes and rivers with their aquatic sediments and landforms, and there are peat bogs and valleys with their terrestrial ones. There is a huge amount and marvellous diversity of archaeological sites and monuments with preservation which is as good as anything to be seen on Dartmoor or in the Wessex downs. Close juxtaposition and lateral movement during their formation have allowed these different strands of evidence to be correlated and a picture of locales to be established. The linear earthworks traversing different kinds of land, the vegetational history of the pollen diagrams at different spatial scales, and the river and lake erosion and sediment histories are especially telling in this respect. As we will see in the next chapter, these land histories can be studied in a broader setting of south-east Scotland and northern England. But this must not blinker us into seeing the establishment of regional schemes as a favoured goal. The beauty of the area is its diversity, and this is not just a diversity of the data but a diversity of human endeavour too.

7 The River Tyne and Hadrian's Wall

We now look at some other parts of northern England and southern Scotland. The area includes the land of Hadrian's Wall (**69**), then south into Durham and north into Northumberland (**73**) and on up to the Antonine Wall. We encompass the Cheviots, but focus our histories more closely on the first millennium BC and the Roman period than we did in the last chapter. First, to set the broader scene, we look at the Tyne Valley.

The River Tyne

Like those of many long river valleys, the histories of the Tyne can be examined by comparing different reaches in terms of topography and distance from the sea. There is the lower part where there is estuarine influence, a middle part, with its two major branches of the North and South Tyne, which is lowlying and broad, and an upper part where the course is steep and in many upland valleys. As you move upstream the areas of influence become increasingly dispersed and localised. Viewed in this way we might isolate factors which relate to these different areas and we can describe different histories and their localities. We must also look not only at the valley bottom and its immediate edges but the whole catchment because this is where the metals, mineral matter and organic material which get into the river and make up its deposits come from. There is also a windblown component of pollen, chemicals and dust from even further afield. Work on the Tyne has been done by Mark Macklin and his co-workers in Newcastle upon Tyne, from which the following account is drawn

In the lower Tyne at Scotswood (**69**), 11 miles upstream from its mouth, and in an area within the present tidal range, there was aggradation of peaty and silty clays c5640/4950-3780/3370 BC as a response to sea-level rise. The deposits, called the Shibdon Unit (**70**), are almost 30ft thick (c+0.15 to -9.0m OD) and formed mainly in freshwater conditions on a floodplain of alder swamp, probably with broad-leaved willows too. Peat overlying this is dated to c3600/3500 BC. This environment was unsuitable for intensive use by humans and even dangerous, especially around the lagg areas at the junction with the valley edge where the ground was very soft. It was difficult to drain, but it could have been used for fowling and other resources like reeds for thatching and alder wood for charcoal.

Still in the lower part of the valley, dynamic fluviatile activity with valley bottom entrenchment took place sometime c3780/3370-970/410 BC, initially perhaps due to a major flood and then by significant channel migration across the floodplain. Alluvium of

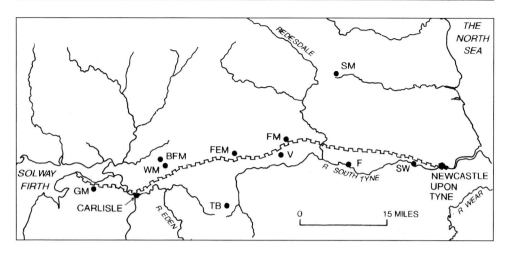

69   *The River Tyne and Hadrian's Wall. BFM, Bolton Fell Moss; F, Farnley; FEM, Fellend Moss; FM, Fozy Moss; GM, Glasson Moss; SM, Steng Moss; SW, Scotswood; TB, Thinhope Burn; WM, Walton Moss; V, Vindolanda*

the Blaydon and Axwell Units partially refilled this incision (**70**). The beginning of this deposition was earlier than the middle of the first millennium BC, as dated by an oak trunk and a wooden wheel from beneath 16ft of sands and clays, while absence of trace metal contamination suggests that it had ceased by the Middle Ages. These deposits are linked to accelerated human disturbance in a land of extensive arable and pasture, but may also be due to increased flood frequencies. A further alluvium, the Scotswood Unit, may be due to higher run-off and increased flooding associated with the Little Ice Age of the sixteenth-nineteenth centuries; the lead content of this alluvium reflects historic mining. From the early seventeenth century onwards, there was downcutting of 16-23ft because of large floods, dredging and channel straightening, and then infilling by alluvium of the Winlaton Unit prior to late nineteenth century channel improvements.

In the Middle Tyne at Farnley Haughs, four alluvial units, each lower than the previous one, were formed by lateral channel shift of a meandering river. Each is made up of sandy gravels with tree trunks (**5**), which are the river-bed and bar material, overlain by finer overbank and slack-water deposits. Deposition started with the Willy Wood Unit, c4940/4600-1350/550 BC. There was major valley-floor incision 1350-550 BC lowering the river bed by more than 6ft, followed by further infilling, the Farnley Unit, 970/410 BC-AD 600/890. Chemical analysis indicates that this material derived almost entirely from the North Tyne, unlike the Willy Wood Unit which comes from both the North and South Tyne, and this tells us something about the relative intensity of agriculture in these two areas. On the floodplain itself, the shifting land and incremental additions of sand, silt and clay would have made it a suitable, if dynamic, medium for agriculture (**p. 88**). So, as in the lower part of the valley there was alluviation, after a period of incision, beginning in the first millennium BC and continuing into the early Middle Ages which was partly coeval with (and inferentially linked to) woodland removal and agricultural

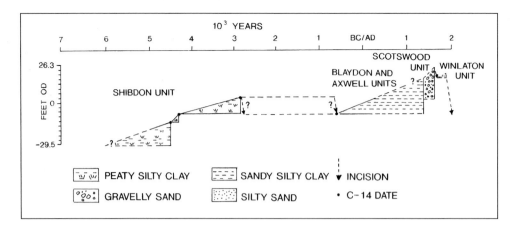

70   *Age-depth diagram of Holocene alluvial units and incision episodes in the lower Tyne at
Scotswood. (Based on Passmore et al. 1992)*

expansion. The Styford Unit is dated by enhanced metal content (lead, zinc and copper), reflecting the beginning of mining in the catchment in the seventeenth century AD. Late eighteenth century downcutting and renewed deposition of coarse material on top of the Styford Unit may have been due to a very large flood documented to 1771.

In the uplands, at Thinhope Burn, there was a meandering channel with relatively slow fine-grained sedimentation until early historic times. In contrast to the middle and lower parts of the valley, these upper reaches did not see major incision until after AD 240/530. The area, at 590-1950ft, takes in land well above the limits of agriculture so there may be a connection between this and the late timing of the onset of downcutting and alluviation. Subsequently there was massive down-cutting, linked to a shift to wetter conditions, and possibly triggered by vegetation disturbance. Renewed alluviation around AD 1450 and channel degradation in the late eighteenth century were associated with unusually high runoff and severe floods. The intermittent character of the downcutting and sedimentation over the last 1600 years has led to the formation of distinct and sharply-cut terraces along the valley sides, and you can see these in upland valleys generally where they provide locations for pasture and the siting of stock enclosures and dwellings (**61**).

Peat bogs

In the middle and later part of the Holocene, many of the earlier lakes had shrunk in size or become completely filled in and developed into peat bogs. In extensive low-lying areas there also developed large areas of raised bog (**p. 23**). There are also many small basin bogs, some only a few hundred yards across (**71**), which began forming in hollows and valleys at various times from the end of the Ice Age right into the historic periods. These peaty areas are called bogs, flows, mires or mosses. You sometimes get the impression that they are unproductive, unfavourably contrasted with drier and more fertile farmland, and that their only use is as a resource for studying vegetational and climate history. But

71   Blackpool Moss, a small basin or topogenous bog in the Scottish Borders

they have provided since their inception, and continue to provide, resources for people, especially at times when agriculture otherwise reduces diversity in the land as a whole. Alder was used for charcoal and constructions, heather for bedding, turves for fuel and animal bedding and the purple moorgrass (*Molinia caerulea*) for rough grazing and even thatching poorer dwellings. Reeds around the pools and lakes were a valuable resource for roofing and flooring. They provided wetlands for fowling and fishing, and the peat itself could be cut for fuel. Management and ownership regimes were often complex, with regular periods of reed-cutting in particular areas so that there was no over-exploitation, and of *Molinia* burning so that the nutrient quality of the vegetation was maintained. Words like 'carr' for alder or birch woodland on peat or 'swamp' for the extensive areas of reeds (*Phragmites*) are not just descriptive: they have a time embeddedness of management implications as well.

Climate change

The vegetation of the mosses is made up of heathy shrubs like the heathers or Ericaceae (*Erica tetralix* and *Calluna*) and crowberry (*Empetrum nigrum*), mosses like *Sphagnum*, *Rhacomitrium* and *Polytrichum*, wetland grasses like purple moor-grass (*Molinia caerulea*), and sedges such as cotton grass (*Eriophorum spp.*). These are patterned across the mire surfaces, with drier areas of heaths and wetter areas of *Sphagnum* and standing water. There were also times when birch and alder colonised the mire surfaces and willows of the broad-leaved kind (rather than the narrow-leaved ones that we may be more familiar with today) grew up in the lagg areas along its edges.

The visible remains of these plants — wood, leaves, fruits and seeds ('macros') — and their microscopic pollen and spores can be used to track the history of mire vegetation. Of especial interest in this respect are those changes which reflect the hydrology, as with the different species of *Sphagnum*, of which some live as hummock-top species (e.g. *S. acutifolia*), others in pools (e.g. *S. cuspidatum*), and yet others in a range of habitats (e.g. *S. imbricatum*). The wetness or dryness of the mire can also be indicated by the degree of humification of the peat and its rate of growth. There may be correlations with known climatic events like the Little Climatic Optimum and Little Ice Age, although burning and draining of the mires may also affect the hydrology. Work at Bolton Fell Moss c5 miles north of Hadrian's Wall (**69**) by Keith Barber and his research team identified periods of increased wetness at AD 810/850, AD 900/1100, AD 1300 with a zenith at 1425, and another at 1780 when there was even open water across the mire. Further work at this

72   *Ribwort plantain*
      (Plantago lanceolata).
      Left: whole plant; right:
      detail of flowers

moss, going back 6300 years and using fine and regular sampling, close C-14 dates and multivariate analysis, showed that wetness changes had a c800-year periodicity. At Talla Moss, 9 miles north of Moffat in the Scottish borders, another group of researchers under Frank Chambers identified several increases of wetness between 1877/1788 BC and AD 1420. There was a suggested cycle of c210 years, which was out of phase with major vegetational changes. Dating, especially correlation with other sites, was difficult, but chemical fingerprinting of volcanic-ash (tephra), of which there were six separate layers, could solve this.

Changes around the bogs

The dryland vegetation from areas surrounding the mires also contributes pollen to the mire surface so their histories too can be followed. These are of more concern to the archaeologists since they reflect human land-use. Thus at Bolton Fell Moss, for almost the whole of the second and first millennia BC there was much woodland and little agriculture, although there was some plantain (**72**) and cereals. In the later half of the first millennium there was a more open land for grazing animals, while in the Roman period, around AD 100, there was a massive increase in dryland grasses (Poaceae), cereals, plantain and *Rumex* which are important indicators of human disturbance. Subsequently there was

a reduction in open land until Scandinavian settlement led to renewed agriculture. Later decreases of activity were correlated with the Border Wars and the Black Death, while there was an increase during the period of the sixteenth-century Border raids.

Hadrian's Wall

By later prehistory there were areas where trees had been removed in the land of Hadrian's Wall. Cord-rig distributions show the extensive nature of prehistoric agriculture in the area **(p. 90)**, with at least twelve sites which are pre-Roman. There were many small peat bogs along the frontier.

Vegetational histories

Following up on their work at Bolton Fell Moss, and to focus specifically on the Roman period, Keith Barber and his team investigated several of these mosses from the area between the Antonine Wall and Hadrian's Wall. The general events were similar to those at Bolton Fell Moss, with minimal impact during the second and first millennia BC, followed by massive deforestation during the Roman invasion and the construction of Hadrian's and the Antonine Walls. The first major clearances could be pinpointed generally to the latest first century BC or earliest first century AD. More precisely, however, it was suggested that these were Roman rather than prehistoric because of the sudden, rather than gradual, increase in clearance indicators and the low level of arable, both of which were correlated with clearance for constructional purposes and pasture. It is all very satisfying, especially the degree of clearance of woodland in the Roman period which was greatest near to the walls where it was seen as reflecting the use in these of massive amounts of timber and turf. Three mosses, Bolton Fell, Walton and Fellend, just a few miles north of Hadrian's Wall (**69**), show this pattern strongly, and the same is true of sites close to the Antonine Wall.

In the last few years, work has been even more intensively focussed on Hadrian's Wall, with increasing specification of ways in which Romans might have used the land. At Bolton Fell Moss and two other mosses close to the Wall, this was done to investigate the 'Roman impact' specifically (**69**). At Walton Moss in Cumbria (2 miles north of the Wall), woodland removal began during the second century BC. At the actual period of invasion there was woodland increase with small clearances, but this was followed by sustained and increasing clearance (cAD 125/395) when Hadrian's Wall was built (AD 122-130). Clearance was linked partly with wall building and later with settled agricultural conditions in the area under Roman presence. At Glasson Moss also in Cumbria (500yds south of the wall) woodland removal may have begun as early as the fourth century BC. It was renewed and accelerated during the Roman period, beginning cAD 125. At Fozy Moss (200yds north of the wall) in Northumbria there was little human impact in prehistory with only small temporary clearings, so the situation here was different from that in the Cumbrian sites; then, cAD 125, the land was almost totally deforested, with cereal pollen indicating arable agriculture. There were several large settlements in the area, and these continued in use during the period when military activity shifted northwards for there was no decline in land-use intensity. At all three sites there was woodland regeneration from the fourth century AD onwards, although this was not very marked at Walton Moss, while later vegetational events were closely related to settlement, war and agriculture.

Questions of dating

In some sites chronology is not very tight, and there is always the possibility that some of these massive clearances may have taken place a few decades before the Roman invasion. The amount of prehistoric ridge cultivation recorded from along the area of the Wall strengthens this suspicion. Even where there is C-14 data, the dating of these major woodland clearances along the line of Hadrian's Wall and in its vicinity to the Roman period has been questioned. Statistically some are most likely pre-Roman and could thus be part of a broader pattern of prehistoric farming expansion, not of military origin at all.

The identification of who was responsible for these particular events is clearly crucial, coming as they do at the junctions between different cultural influences. C-14 is considered by some to be valueless in this, as being too imprecise, but fine sampling of peat at millimetre intervals, AMS dates, refined wiggle-matching and Bayesian calibration might all be successfully applied.

Another approach is to use pollen sequences and other environmental data that have been precisely dated by dendrochronology and archaeology, and the examples of two first-century AD Roman forts, Carlisle and Vindolanda, are relevant here (**69**).

Carlisle is towards the western end and just 600yds to the south of Hadrian's Wall, on a low promontory of boulder clay above alluvium of the Rivers Eden and Caldew. There was a fort there in early Roman times, established in AD 72 (**82**), so 50 years or so before the building of Hadrian's Wall in AD 122. The defences were of timber and turf, and excavations have yielded large quantities of timber dated by dendrochronology. This has allowed specific elements of pre-Roman and Roman land-use to be tied in precisely to historical events, and the work of Mike McCarthy has contributed significantly to this debate. South of the fort the Roman town of Luguvalium was established in the AD 80s. Both the fort and the town were built in pasture or woodland pasture, although there were large areas of alder woods, probably on the floodplains. Some of the buildings and their properties were defined by hedges of blackthorn or wild cherry (*Prunus*). Oak used for structural timbers was mainly from trees that began life in the second or first centuries BC (79% of a sample of 246). In other words they were relatively young and this could imply previous clearance of woodlands on quite a large scale. Alder was used abundantly for wall infill, drain linings, hurdles and fences. A large variety of other species was also exploited, and it looks as if there was considerable use of woodlands around Carlisle several decades if not centuries before Hadrian's Wall was built. The source of the various cereal and domestic animal species used by the inhabitants is unknown, but was probably local, and we can refer again to the prehistoric cord-rig close by **(p. 97)**. Insect remains indicate a diversity of habitats including hay, disturbed ground, peat, heathland and pasture, and that the Romans were importing bedding, animal feed and possibly roofing materials.

Vindolanda is another fort which has produced significant botanical data. It is on the Stanegate about a mile to the south of the Wall, close to some of the highest ground of the Wall, at c525ft OD, and just over 3 miles south-west of Fozy Moss. Roman presence dates from the late AD 70s/early 80s, slightly later than at Carlisle, but significantly earlier than the building of the Wall in the AD 120s/130s. The fort has a complicated history and archaeological dating of some of the periods is precise, more or less to individual years. Earlier forts were of timber, mostly birch, suggesting an already cleared land; oak timbers had been seasoned and possibly imported. The preservation of posts, log rafts and wattle fences in the ditches is superb. Later forts were of stone. Usefully, the pollen assemblages reflect the local contemporary vegetation, not just that of the ditches themselves, and there seems to be little re-worked pollen. The earlier of the two ditch fills sampled were Period I ponded organic sediments, mostly clays, and dated to cAD 85-92. Woodland had been cleared from the area before cAD 85, perhaps by native farmers rather than the Roman military, but certainly nothing to do with the Wall. Alder was the only locally-growing tree and otherwise only scrub remained. Herbs associated with wet meadow or pasture, like broad-leaved dock (*Rumex obtusifolia*), and the scarcity of heath plants suggest heavy grazing and, more widely, an expanding agrarian economy perhaps, in the absence of cereals, specialised towards cattle. The name Vindolanda is a Romanised form of Celtic meaning 'white lawns' or 'white enclosed land'. A later sequence, mainly organic sands and clays, came from the Period VI ditch dated cAD 160-180. Here, clearance also occurred early in the second century AD, probably in an expansion of land for grazing, followed by possible cereal cultivation in the early- to mid-second century. Again alder was the only local tree, and again heath plants were unimportant. So the ditch deposits of the fort at Vindolanda, dating precisely to the start of Roman occupation, show there had already been substantial removal of woodland resources at least half a century before the construction of Hadrian's Wall, that there was extensive pasture, that it was not for military purposes and that there was no cereal cultivation until the mid-second century.

The wider scene

In the later half of the first millennium BC there was a variable impact of people on the land, with some areas showing more intensive and longer-lasting clearances as early as the fourth century (400/350 BC), while in others these did not begin until the second and first centuries (c200/150 BC). This was all quite different in its intensity, rapidity and scale from earlier small clearances, with burning and soil erosion a more integral part. But there were still some areas which showed a continuation of the earlier small temporary clearances and minimal change in woodland cover right up to the Roman period.

Variations in timing need to be considered in terms of each moss or pollen catchment, not just because there are variable taphonomies (especially catchment area in relation to basin size) but because of variations in the local conditions of soils, altitude and human business. While clearances were often for pasture and sometimes for cereal cultivation there are other possibilities, like the establishment of settlements or areas for mineral exploitation and stone quarrying. Shrines, of which there are several along the line of the Hadrianic frontier, may also have opened up the woodland locally. The Wall is often on high land, going up to almost 1000ft OD, and there are some spectacular crags and cliffs above which it is built. So some woodland decline could have been the result of animal activity around these in the same way as we discussed for Dartmoor **(p. 26)**, with their foci then becoming sacred places of the Brigantes and Carvetti.

A corollary of these possible different purposes for clearance is that although some show a general synchroneity, there is no evidence that they occurred precisely at the same time. They may have been diachronous and site specific, and with no precise correlation between intensity, sharpness and style. Indeed, in some areas woodland regeneration had even begun prior to the Roman invasion. The only regional pattern may have been one of diversity in timing and course. This needs to be remembered.

Crop husbandries

Still in the area of Hadrian's Wall but more widely to the north and south (**73**), Marijke van der Veen looked at land-use of later prehistory and the early Roman period from the point of view of crop husbandry. She analysed specifically the macro-remains of the arable weeds which characterise different types of soil and land-use, and from a number of settlements identified different regimes (table 7.1). There were two main sorts, essentially reflecting differences north and south of the River Tyne.

Table 7.1 Two kinds of crop husbandry and their signals at settlements, based on the work of van der Veen, with notes from R Tipping and G Ferrell.

GROUP 'A' SITES — Chester House, lowland Northumberland, rectilinear; Murton High Crags and West Dod Law, Northumberland uplands, curvilinear, ramparted, communal

Main crop: emmer
Subsidiary crops: spelt and barley
Arable weeds: intensive soil working, weeding and manuring, and fertile soil
Regime: intensive, small-scale and high labout input
Settlements: defended and isolated
Distribution: coastal plain and uplands north of the R. Tyne
Tribal affinity: isolated communities of the Votadini
Tipping comments: intensely conservative, less central
Expected pollen signal: small temporary clearances or low level of clearance and activity

GROUP 'B' SITES — Rock Castle, North Yorkshire, rectilinear; Thorpe Thewles, Cleveland, rectilinear, developing into a large, complex open settlement second/first centuries BC; Stanwick, an oppidum **(p. 108)**

Main crops: Spelt and barley
Arable weeds: limited soil working and manuring, and less fertile soil
Regime: extensive, larger areas and low labour input
Settlements: non-defended and integrated
Distribution: R. Tees lowlands
Tribal affinity: integrated communities of the Brigantes
Tipping comments: linked to a more centralised political system which encouraged the expansion of large-scale agriculture
Expected pollen signal: clearances and activity more widespread

---

In the group 'A' sites, agriculture was intensive but on a small-scale; it could persist unchanged, as at Hallshill in Redesdale, for many centuries. In the group 'B' sites, fields were less intensively managed but the system was more flexible in that larger areas could be taken in; it was linked to a more centralised political system which encouraged expansion.

In considering the pollen evidence from these two areas, however, Tipping does away with the harsh regionality of van der Veen's two husbandries. In its place he sees a wider occurrence in the later first millennium of extensive farming systems throughout northern England and southern Scotland. Although there are differences in the sorts of data being used, it is still claimed that the pollen undermines the idea, especially, of small-scale intensive strategies in the northern part of the study area north of the Tyne.

Spatial organisation
Gill Ferrell took things up from the point of view of spatial organisation both within and between the settlements. She suggested that particular spatial and architectural styles of settlement were related to specific socialities, land and husbandry. Sites which were mainly in the Northumberland uplands, including the hillfort of Yeavering, sites in the

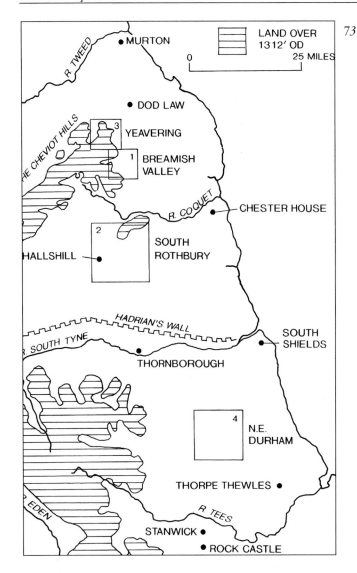

73 *Sites of macroscopic plant remains used by van der Veen (1992) (round black dots) and the study areas of Ferrell (1997) (numbered squares)*

Breamish Valley in the northern and eastern Cheviots, and those in South Rothbury to the south (**73**) constituted one group. The similar size of these sites, their enclosed or defended nature and their many buildings indicated a loose, non-integrated and un-ranked organisation of large extended families, each with high autonomy and isolation from other groups (**43, 65**). Only Yeavering Bell, a hillfort of 13ac (5.3ha) and containing 130 circular buildings, was outside the mean size range of these settlements. Sites of van der Veen's group 'A' husbandries, intensive and conservative, are included in this type. In contrast, sites in north-east Durham, a more lowland area, were of a greater range of sizes and with fewer buildings, suggesting a more ranked society and a developed, integrated, settlement system. Perhaps significantly in this respect, the Stanwick oppidum (**p. 108**) is 12.5 miles to the south. Here are the group 'B' sites which, with their more extensive strategies linked to a wide political system, encouraged expansion of agriculture.

What is it all about?

In an overview, Marijke van der Veen and Terry O'Connor see these changes of agriculture in later prehistory and the Roman period as part of a growing regionalisation. A notable feature was the creation of settlements which were not primarily involved in agricultural production - hillforts, oppida, Roman forts and towns. In contrast to the expansion of agriculture up to the middle of the first millennium BC which is seen as a function of growing populations, subsequent growth was a response to the development of social stratification, the emergence of non-agricultural segments of the population and their need for food. This required increasing productivity in existing areas of farming (intensification) or extending the area farmed without increasing the labour force (extensification).

Changes in the use of particular crop and animal types were a part of this. There was a shift from emmer wheat to spelt in later prehistory, and from these to bread wheat in the Roman period. The shift to spelt is related to tolerance of heavier soils, hardiness (it can be winter sown) and higher yields, allowing movement onto new soil types and a more flexible sowing regime. Regional patterns are identified, as in the north-east. Animal bones suggest a shift from sheep to cattle in the Roman period which correlates with an increased emphasis on cereals since cattle are the least efficient of the three main domesticates for rapid meat production and are needed for ploughing. Again there are differences that are regional and related to site type. Roman military sites have predominantly cattle whereas prehistoric and Roman sites in less Romanised areas have higher proportions of sheep. Villas and later Roman sites have higher proportions of pig than do native and earlier Roman sites. There are some indications that the shift to cattle began in later prehistory but this was countered at some very late prehistoric sites where an increase in sheep took place.

This kind of structured approach is very different from the one that I have been advocating. Things are sorted out in terms of broad schemes, of possibilities to the need for change, of psychology vs. practicality in choosing and adopting new strategies, and of differences between intensification and extensification. Then, too, it is all dutifully accommodating, seeing extensification and intensification as extremes in a continuum, as not being mutually exclusive at all but as being able to occur on the same farm and adopted severally as conditions require or allow. The approach is also explicitly progressional, focussing on and accepting expansion and regionalisation, almost as inevitable, and with references to the 'need' for expansion implying external cause. The concept of 'surplus' implies a clear break between the farming and the non-farming communities; but if food production is integrated with demands then it is not surplus. This is not trivial semantics. It is crucial to how we should be looking at the relationships of agricultural and non-agricultural communities.

Against these criticisms, however, there is much interesting detail in the van der Veen & O'Connor analysis about the mechanisms whereby these different kinds of land-use developed. In sites of both groups, barley was grown on the poorer soils and thus under more extensive conditions than wheat, highlighting the differences in status of the two crops and showing that different approaches to expansion could take place on the same farm. In this flexibility, slight changes in climate or labour conditions could shift the balance between the two crops, and this may have been without any express decision on the part of the farmer. The practice of sowing mixed crops of emmer and spelt also leant itself to natural selection under changes in soil quality. Changes in crop types, as from glume to free-threshing wheats, and the ways in which animals, dung and fodder were moved around over the land led to different practices of processing, storage and distribution. And not least, this flexibility leant itself to manipulation through expression, in the creation of new localities. Granaries, for example, could be sited to express wealth and power. You can see this today where barns are positioned so that they are well visible as you approach the farm, while the farmhouse itself is not seen until you are almost there. Of course aeration vs. shelter, respectively, may have a lot to do with this as well.

Engagement

> 'Would you come cutting furze with me
> Mary Malone?'
>
> 'I would and I would bind with you
> My darling and my own!'
>
> *Irish song* (from AT Lucas, *Furze*)

Communities are maintained in the first instance as localities — interactions between people and people and between them and their surrounds. Whatever upheavals were going on in politics, climate or demography, or whatever gradual shifts were taking place in crops, soils or religion, their translation into change or changelessness always took place as localities. There is, however, a tendency to use overarching schemes as frameworks for interpretation without putting in this analytical stage. Interpretation needs both, not least because this was how people led their lives.

Polarities

Polarities are especially damaging. These can be the focussing on particular horizons as defined by distinctive events, like the fall in elm pollen in the early fourth millennium BC or the building of Hadrian's Wall in the AD 120s; they can be the creation of contrasts like the micro-regions of lowland arable and upland pasture in the northern Cheviots or the different crop husbandries of north-east England; or they can refer to oppositions of interpretation as with climate vs. people in river-valley processes and soil erosion, or natives vs. Romans in the clearing of woodland.

There is nothing intrinsically wrong with polarities; this is one of the ways we give order to our lives today and it was no doubt so in the past. The problem is the link with practice, or lack of it; if we start with polarities, we miss important links between data and behaviour.

Causation

Once we look for cause, we are polarising our ideas when cause may be difficult to define, let alone identify, and even not so important at all. In this fall in the elm pollen, for example — what we call '*the* elm decline' when in fact there can be several — , we discuss the relative merits of diseases, human clearance or other sorts of impact, or climate. But the key issue is what was going on in terms of the elms and the land and people, and how changes were encompassed in future ecologies **(p. 85)**. It is the same with fire **(p. 39)**.

Questions of causation often focus on strikingly visible effects, like the remains of abandoned settlements in marginal land or terraces in river valleys, and the identification of a few agencies, especially climate, human land-use and geomorphology. But these abstractions are made up of many inter-related aspects. Subsistence farms, for example, were mixed, spatially variable and temporally flexible in their strategies. There was a complex interplay between farming, land and climate. Manuring and moving cattle around into different feeding areas were related to vegetation quality and growth, and these in turn to winter temperatures and frosts. Vegetation and animals affected geomorphology while the enclosure of land with walls and hedges or the clearing of woodland affected local climate. Such farms were also often non-maximising, so climate was not necessarily a constraint. At least there was a mean level of crop rotation, variations in proportions of particular livestock, and movement to and from particular areas of outlying land which was seldom exceeded. On the whole people did the same thing one year they did the last. Any idea that changes were caused by climate must take this complexity and flexibility on board, must show how farmers were affected by climate change, and must show how human response interfaced with it.

Importantly, there was an interplay of human expression in a community through the biophysical environment. For example, gorse or furze (*Ulex europaeus*), provides many needs: AT Lucas in his book on *Furze* (1960) itemises well over thirty for Ireland. And in these the gorse may have been exploited by different groups. For fuel for making pots and cooking it may have been collected by women; for temporary barricades in animal control it was more likely collected by men; as fodder for horses it may have been the preserve of a young male elite; while in its place of growth, where it may have been deliberately planted, it provided valuable browse for animals in the community generally **(74)**. Old gorse is burnt today *in situ* in Mynydd Preseli and along the coast in west Wales to improve its palatability for grazing, but this of course destroys its use for fuel. Pressures on any of these areas of exploitation could lead to a shift in the power network within a community with knock-on effects for its structure and practice. It might, for example, have little effect if a balance went in favour of the men and the use of gorse for fuel were prohibited. The women would burn animal dung instead, bringing the cattle and sheep nearer to the farmstead and perhaps ultimately increasing their importance in the economy. On the other hand, it could be serious if its use for horse fodder were forbidden. The young males would move away, impoverishing the community's work-force and leading to serious stresses at times of harvest and land tillage.

At one level, these tensions are primarily about different uses of gorse. Where there were interactions with other resources as where gorse occurred in proximity to moles, the situation is more complex. The moles could be seen variously as a valuable resource

74   *Gorse in the Brecon Beacons*

for their fur, as improving the soils and vegetation or as destructive and wicked, so the fate of the gorse may depend on the meanings that were given to the moles. But this is all still about practicalities. At another level, things could be related to interactions among different groups within the community in terms of gender, identity or power, or between individuals as expressions of love, and not primarily about gorse at all, although gorse is still the medium through which these interactions are played out. Yet more complex is the situation where struggles of gender through the use of gorse could have interfaced with meanings of land which themselves were related to the expressive order, irrespective of whether gorse was growing there or not. An area where gorse was growing that was accessible only to women would become disused if women were banned from using gorse.

Thus causation can have many levels while responses can be spread over a wide time-range from the instantaneous to the almost infinitely delayed. In the desertion of upland settlements there can be a whole range of events, like vegetation being cleared, soils becoming impoverished, people going back to the same area because of good grazing land or ancestral sacredness, or interplays of power or gender through resources, like gorse and moles, before there was a permanent shift of settlement. Climate or land-use or geomorphology may be an influence, but only a trigger after a long period of change.

However, one area where a unilineal relationship between causes and effects *is* relevant is where these were perceived as such in the past. Changes in river courses, for instance, can take place quite rapidly as seen in comparisons of successive meander positions from nineteenth century tithe maps, later maps and aerial photographs. If climate or human activity were important social issues, as they are today, and people saw either of them as being responsible for such river-valley changes, as they may have done with mining spoil **(p. 74)**, their responses may have been related to feelings like achievement or guilt and these could be relevant to how the land was to be used in the future. If, on the other hand, humans perceived the changes but without any understanding of their causes or even an awareness that their causes were significant, then their response may have been of a more practical kind.

Regionality and progression

Another polarity is the way we look for patterns in data, as in the identification of regionality. Some features, like the Dartmoor reeves and the Scottish brochs, may have had a synchronous history (more or less) over wide areas. They may be truly regional. Other field archaeology, like upland farmsteads, may have originated at different times, one-by-one and here and there, over several decades or centuries even, and although they look like a regional pattern this is only a present-day pattern of archaeology. In the settlement of a small upland valley each farmstead may have had its own history and chronology. And even where there was synchroneity, patterns may be unrelated to a common cause: imposing regionality leads to ideas about regional causation.

Progression is a part of this, with a tendency to see patterns as becoming increasingly marked with time. Instead of entertaining the possibility that communities or cultures were all equally well adapted we tend to see differences as reflecting progress, especially if there is an end point like Hadrian's Wall or the present day. But we cannot equate sparse material culture, sluggishness in adopting new metalworking technology, and conservatism in farming with cerebral inactivity or low economic drive. People could have been doing all sorts of things in woodland with their animals as well as running them in pasture, with a complex system of semi-nomadic life, with complex kinship, residence and exchange. They could have been creating wonderful sagas. And even where we can identify technological progress, as with more hygienic pottery, new kinds of crops, or new art forms, the *use* of these may have been in entirely the opposite direction, and no more intelligent than is often our use of cars, television or the land. Cars mean that we do not have to plan ahead, television that we can spend our evenings being reactive not creative, and land technology that we can escape from a knowledge of how to survive. This is not nostalgia. It is about detraining our brains.

8 Oppida

'We are talking about a big area of land. It includes at least six known Roman villas and their land, most of Blenheim, most of Ditchley, and much of Cornbury, which is another huge estate . . . To put it another way, the rampart encloses a long stretch of the Evenlode valley, four or five separate modern villages, and some varied country, including hills and valleys, heath, forest, stone quarries and river meadows that flood in winter.'

Peter Levi (1983), *The shades of Autumn*, on the Oxfordshire Grim's Dyke

Oppidum was a name given by Julius Caesar to a type of defended prehistoric enclosure and settlement which he found in use during his campaigns in Gaul and Britain. As such, the name refers to sites experienced by Caesar and classified by him as such, and strictly should be confined to such sites. This however would be too rigid but it serves to emphasise that oppida are sites perceived in a particular political and military environment and that they cannot be characterised by archaeological features. They are defined by their historical context.

Oppida were established as defended settlements with many houses in them, and some may have been the seats of tribal chiefs. After that they may have been added to, with activities other than just dwelling, such as smithing and other artisanries, developing within their bounds. If they were suitably sited along navigable rivers or substantially utilised roads then they sometimes formed the nuclei of future towns. Otherwise they may have become deserted. So in addition to the characteristics as seen and established by people who wrote about them there are their functions as originally conceived and those which came later into which they developed. This, of course, is true of any site, natural feature or institution, as Stuart Piggott describes for the Druids, the priests of the oppida. But it is especially true of dense settlements with buildings and fortifications because they are so suited to continued use. On origins, John Collis is pretty dogmatic: '. . . between the Early La Tène hillforts and the Late La Tène Oppida some fundamental changes had taken place in Iron Age society to allow undertakings on a large scale . . .' Some people see these as related to economic pressures, others to changes in kinship structure, yet others to an increasing relationship between farmsteads and non-agricultural settlements and the emergence of local power. Collis is equally positive on their relation to future towns: 'Self-imposition, the construction of massive enclosure for defence, is the way in which urbanisation started in temperate Europe . . .'

Oppida in Britain are few and mainly in the south-east — Hengistbury Head, Colchester, Verlamion (**75**). Stanwick near Darlington in north Yorkshire extends the

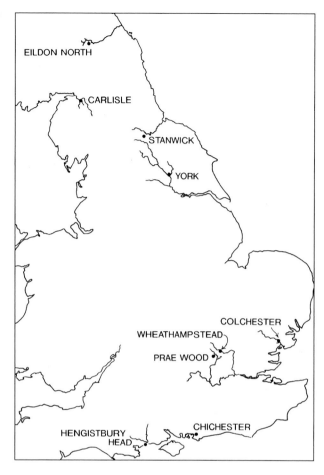

75 *Sites mentioned in chap. 8*

distribution into the north, but it is isolated and late, cAD 50-70, although may be with pre-Claudian settlement as shown by recent work by Colin Haselgrove and associates. It lies between the Rivers Swale and Tees and is just to the west of Scots Dyke, a fragmented linear earthwork which may have formerly linked the two rivers (**76**). Its banks enclose 850ac (344ha) including a smaller complex called the Tofts, a stream and some small hills, and they are clearly of several periods. Pre-oppidum enclosures or fields were probably incorporated and prehistoric agriculture goes back well prior to the first century AD. Geophysical survey and excavation of the Tofts have shown the presence of extensive occupation with several smaller enclosures and circular houses being established prior to the construction of the main earthworks and prior to the importation into the area of Roman fine-wares and roofing tiles; these, in turn, preceded Roman occupation of the area in AD 71-4. Mortimer Wheeler who worked on the site in the 1950s saw the oppidum for keeping animals in under siege. But he chose to play down the fact that it is in prime agricultural land. It is also close to metal ores and there is evidence of high-quality metalworking; and it is at a natural communication junction for north-south and trans-Pennine travel. In addition to keeping domestic animals, the people of the oppidum were hunting red deer, roe deer and hare; and they kept dogs. There were

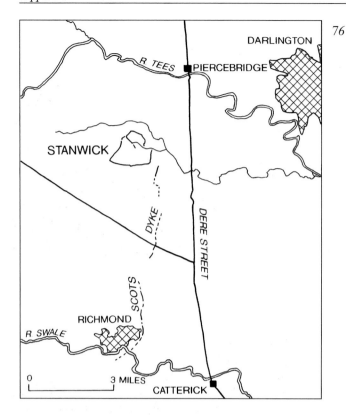

76 *Stanwick.*
Cross-hatched =
modern towns;
black square =
Roman towns.
(Based on
Haselgrove et al.
1990)

sheep-shears and, in waterlogged deposits in a ditch, a sword scabbard, a wooden bowl and basketwork. The siting of Stanwick could thus be related to a number of factors, singly or in combination.

Further north there are sites sometimes classified as 'minor oppida' like Eildon North (**77, 78**) which was once seen as a tribal capital of the Selgovae of the immediate pre-Roman period, although its earliest enclosure dates back to c1000 BC. In this respect, we can recall the Cheviot forts and the way in which their building was sometimes pre-empted at the convergence of linear earthworks (**p. 89**). Eildon North is an odd site in terms of settlement since, with well over 500 houses, there are likely to have been hundreds of people occupying it at some times; yet it was exposed, with steep access and no obvious major water supply. It is a prominent hill with equally prominent views from it, especially of the even more dramatic Middle Hill; and the rock is a distinctive vesicular volcanic material with a pink-red colour. There is good agricultural land all around.

In the south, Hengistbury Head lay within areas of subsistence farms and settlements, with the hillfort area of Dorset to the west, open settlements in central Hampshire, and another hillfort area in the south also with small farming settlements. There was no centralisation of power and at no time was Hengistbury more than an economic centre. It was mostly concerned with importing wine amphorae from the continent in the first half of the first century BC, and was also an iron-working centre based on the local ores.

Some sites like the Oxfordshire Grim's Dyke (**p. 108**) and Chichester (**79**) saw large tracts of land — several square miles — enclosed by dykes. In both these examples, as with

77   *The Eildon Hills. The North Hill with the fort is on the right*

78   *On the summit of Eildon North, with the Middle Hill in the background*

others, water courses were incorporated into and used as a part of the land enclosure. This may have been the situation for Verlamion and Wheathampstead in Hertfordshire where a short length of dyke may be the remnants of a once more complete system linking the two sites and the land between the Rivers Lea and Ver (**80**). The individual sites may both have used a river and its floodplain as a fourth side. In addition to the main oppidum of Verlamion, there are three rectangular and subdivided small enclosures incorporated

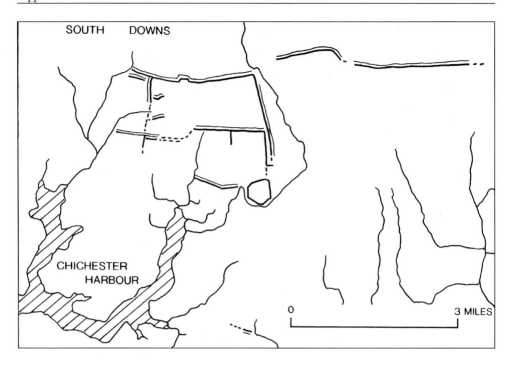

79   *Chichester earthworks. Note the general location between the South Downs and Chichester Harbour, and the incorporation of rivers into the system. (Based on Bradley 1971)*

within the complex. One of these, Gorhambury, included a settlement, cAD 20-43, which continued into the Roman period until cAD 350. The adjacent stretch of oppidum bank was built after the Gorhambury settlement had been in use for several years, in the latest years of prehistory; and other enclosures and settlements nearby may also have been earlier than the oppidum as part of the rural settlement, and thus incorporated into its aegis. Animal compounding is a likely function of the major dykes as they define rich meadow in the valley floor and seem unsuitable for defence.

There was a prehistoric cemetery associated with Verlamion, c10/1 BC-AD 40/50, just to the north-east of Prae Wood at King Harry Lane, with 455 cremations and 17 inhumations. The cremations were mostly in pots and 87 had accompanying animal bones. Some of them were situated within rectilinear ditched enclosures, a burial at the centre of each with large numbers of grave goods, seen as a founder, less rich ones around (**81**). There was a decrease in unburnt grave goods through time which, if these were items of the mourners and not the deceased, reflects the size of individual social networks to which the deceased belonged; amphorae, reflecting long-distance alliances, were often with the central graves. Burials outside the enclosures are seen as late and as belonging to newcomers who looked to contacts within the oppidum in the stead of the former more extensive kin networks.

Later, in the second century AD at Gorhambury they were skinning dogs.

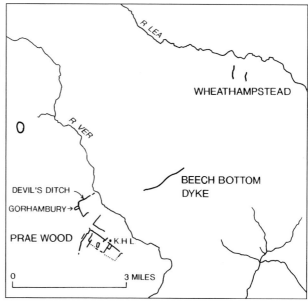

80   *Wheathampstead and Verlamion (Prae Wood and Devils Ditch). (Based on Haselgrove & Millett /1997)*

Oppida distribution and siting must be understood at different scales and levels of meaning. Collis sees oppida in a land of small subsistence farms but they may have served a more mobile agro-pastoralist type of economy where herds of cattle and maybe sheep were moved around the land, with settlements left and taken up again over periods of a few months or several years. The complexities of the earthworks on some of the sites may have lent them to the sorting of stock as suggested by Francis Pryor for some of the earlier and much smaller enclosures of the Fens **(p. 42)**. The earthworks of the Prae Wood site of the Verulamium oppidum really are incredibly complex. Intermittent use of oppida is best seen in the construct of semi-nomadic agro-pastoralism, as suggested by Wheeler for Stanwick, and, in coastal areas, this may have been integrated with other industries like salting as Richard Bradley has proposed.

Additionally, there were social and craft groupings at least in northern European if not in British oppida, with upper-class houses in secluded areas and workshops and shops along the main streets. There was abundant iron-working, manufacture of pottery and glass, and coinage as at Verlamion, with the proximity of iron ores and ecological diversity being important, while agricultural land was of low significance. There was widespread trade at local and pan-European scales, and siting seems to have related to trade routes substantially. The southern English oppida are seen as being related to the development of external competitive marketing and as being sited in relation to communications. For specific locations, defence was paramount in Europe, only rarely being overridden by economic factors as in the case of salt production. In eastern England, in contrast, few sites were in a defensive situation, although specific earthwork positionings may have been related to this as at Stanwick. In some cases, Stanwick again and Eildon North, local positionings may have been dictated by earlier land-use. In others it may have been status, as at Verlamion, with the visible impressiveness of the earthworks themselves being the relevant factor. In yet others, siting may have been related to the ritual significance of rivers

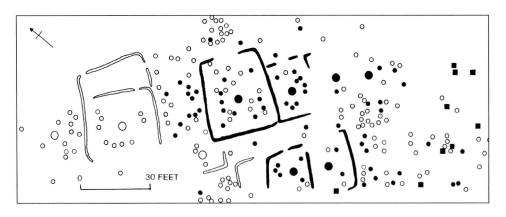

81   *Verlamion, King Harry Lane cemetery. Black dots and enclosures = phase 1; open = phase 3; squares = phase 4a. (Based on Stead & Rigby 1989)*

and marshes and there may be a link with important natural and cultural boundaries. The idea that oppida were set in liminal land, used at once as meeting places and places of mediation between agricultural and less tamed land, has parallels with brochs which were being built in the north and west at about the same time **(p. 60)**.

An interesting question, as always, is: 'Why this particular form of bio-physical expression, why oppida?' However diverse their meaning, there is still — like with the causewayed camps before them and the brochs — this biophysical uniformity.

> 'Few oppida seem to be at the centre of differentiated settlement networks of the kind usually associated with urbanism, and few display a higher level of intra-site zoning than do rural farms or hamlets' — (Woolf 1993)

On the contrary, many are in areas which had been little exploited previously, suggesting expansion into marginal land. This does, however, recall the locations of the much earlier causewayed camps of the fourth millennium BC where a function as meeting places for several different groups in neutral ground was proposed. It is easy to see some of the extensive hillfort and linear-earthwork complexes of the Cheviots and Lammermuir Hills as serving the same function but lacking just the formality of the large encirclements. Even Caesar included some hillforts with no urban characters as oppida. Indeed, there may have been oppida without earthworks at all, with just the place being important. Woodland may have been cleared prior to their construction in some cases, like with the causewayed camps, and this, too, lends itself to the idea that clearances alone may have sufficed, although perhaps manipulated with huge barricades of gorse. And there was no shortage of woodland clearances — as we know from the pollen diagrams!

Oppida thus served various functions, probably several at a time, articulating space, movement of animals and human relationships like power and magic.

9 Roman towns

Carlisle

Several towns have organic and other environmental materials going back into the Roman period, with considerable detail of species and locales. Carlisle is one of the better known (**69, 82**). The site is lowlying, although above the River Eden floodplain, and on boulder clay, so there is high quality preservation of wood, timber and other organic materials **(p. 98)**. There was fourth millennium BC activity with three stone axeheads from Great Langdale in the Lake District and a leaf-shaped arrowhead. Ploughmarks in a soil sealed by a turfline underneath Roman levels may belong to any period up to the end of prehistory. A Roman fort was established in AD 72-3, continuing in use until cAD 320/330. A Roman *civitas* (or civilian) settlement, Luguvalium, was begun in AD 79, and this is seen in ribbon development along roads south of the fort. There has been more or less continuous occupation since then, beginning with the construction of buildings and pits and with further activity of buildings fronting onto metalled roads. All this was well prior to Hadrian's Wall which runs through the suburb of Stanwix immediately to the north of the medieval castle.

Work has been done particularly under the supervision of Mike McCarthy. In the *civitas*, at Blackfriar's St (**82**), the buildings were rectangular, c13-16.4ft wide and 46-65ft long with their short sides fronting the street, up to 6.5ft apart and sometimes abutting. There was flooring of earth and clay, patterns of joists, post impressions and floorboard nails. There were some beautiful enamelled objects, glass vessels, window glass, and a cornelian intaglio. Bronze animal heads included one of a dolphin, one of a lion-head terminal on a stud, and one of a pair of horses heads on a key. The Samian ware too was rich in animal motifs, probably of hunting scenes and metaphor. These Romans were in the mainstream of culture and they were wealthy. Settlement continued into late-Roman and immediately post-Roman times with the same area being used for repeated buildings, although with breaks in activity. The buildings were initially for domestic use, but later ones may have been warehouses or workshops.

Insects from the Roman deposits were mainly grain beetles, *Oryzaephilus surinamensis*, *Cryptolestes ferrugineus* and *Sitophilus granarius*, with a few other species which are characteristic of stored products like *Tenebrio obscurus* and *Tenebroides mauritanicus*; *Aglenus brunneus* and *Tipnus unicolor* were also present. Apart from the grain infestations, the assemblage suggests that the deposits formed in reasonably clean conditions, and this seems typical of Roman urban sites, whatever the context. Lack of floor deposits suggests that the buildings were kept clean although there were piles of ash and silts in some areas. Other habitats on the site or nearby reflected in the beetle species were dead wood, water, marsh, foul rotting matter, dung, legumes and crucifers, and open ground, according well with the plant remains. A heath component in the plant remains may represent the gathering of heather for fuel or bedding.

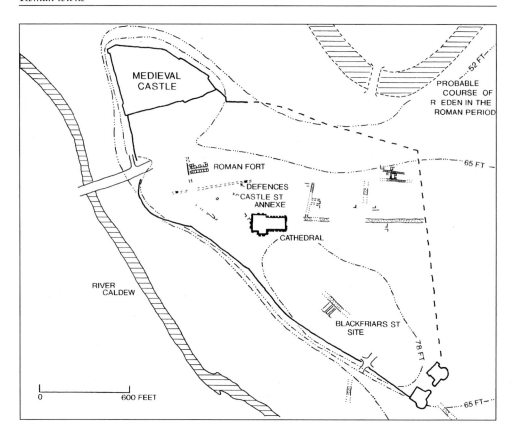

82   *Carlisle; medieval fortifications and the Roman buildings and roads of the second century: (Based on McCarthy 1990)*

    The Roman deposits accumulated to depths of over 3ft. There was, however, no dark earth **(p. 127)**, even though there seems to have been a hiatus of several centuries between the end of Roman occupation and the beginning of Anglian settlement.

    Another excavation was at Castle St, immediately to the south of, and in an annexe to, the fort **(82)**. Here, there was an initial military occupation with buildings, periods 3-6, followed by periods 7-9 which reflect more settled occupation perhaps of non-military type. Environmental evidence was considered by period and in the contrasts between inside and outside of buildings. There were also considerable timber remains which allowed dendrochronological and woodland-use analyses to be made. A major significance of this site was the potential for examining fine spatio-temporal relationships between people and locales at different scales. The quality of the data for this is superb. These are some of the different scales:

1. Britain itself in Roman times was at the edge of the known world and this would have been realised by its inhabitants. The northern location of Carlisle and its proximity to the frontier zone, even though Hadrian's Wall had not been built at the time of the earlier settlement, would have added to this perception of peripherality.

2. Roman Britain, too, saw the intimate association of native and occupier communities, and among the latter there was a huge diversity of ethnic groupings. This was especially so in towns and large military settlements. Perceptions of environment and its use would have varied, partly in relation to traditions, partly to place in the community, and so on.

3. More locally, Carlisle — Luguvalium — was from early on a close juxtaposition of the military and civilian, so there would have been different goals and practicalities among its inhabitants as well as different life views. The Castle Street site itself was even more intimately lodged in this dichotomy, being an annexe to the fort and thus in a dynamic state and where rapid changes of function took place.

4. The sequence of wood and timber use allowed the expression of inter-relationships between different groups of people in the kind of complex ways which we have looked at earlier for gorse **(p. 105)**. These could have been played out in land holdings, methods and partitioning of woodland management and the selection of wood in terms of species, age, size and whether it was coppiced or from branches of a main trunk. Further localities could have been established in perceptions of the uses to which the wood was to be put, transportation from woodlands to the settlement and in the construction of the buildings and their different parts.

5. The contrast between street frontages and the yard areas, or 'backlands', between inside and outside areas, and the diversity of building function and the rooms within the buildings in close proximity allow the possibilities of further analysis of community and individual use.

Prehistoric and Roman York

The rest of this chapter is mainly about the environment of Roman York **(83)**. For the archaeology, I have used Richard Hall's book, *York*, while for the environments I have plundered the detailed writings on insects, plants and bones by Harry Kenward, Alan Hall and Terry O'Connor.

Before the Romans came, there was likely an oppidum there. The area is border country between two Celtic tribes, the Brigantes to the north and west, the Parisii to the east and south, and accordingly there was not a great deal of settlement in the area in the first century BC. There is a short section of dyke, Green Dykes, between two valleys, the location is a plateau between two rivers, the Ouse and the Foss, and there is a flat marshy area to the east which would have provided at once a natural boundary and a place of sacredness and magic. One reading of the name the Romans gave to their settlement in the first century AD, Eboracum, is from the Celtic 'the place of the yew'. The pre-Roman soil was poorly organic, well-drained and not especially subject to flooding. Beetles and plant remains from both sides of the River Ouse — at Skeldergate, Tanner Row and Coney St — show that prior to Roman settlement the banks of the river were rough pasture with bare patches. This is indicated by ribwort plantain (*Plantago major*), parsley piert (*Aphanes arvensis*), knotgrass (*Polygonum aviculare*) and toad-rush (*Juncus bufonius*) **(84)**, with dung beetles (especially *Aphodius* spp.), and the influence of aquatic and water-edge habitats. Assemblages with a superabundance of the grassland snail *Vallonia excentrica* from near Tanner Row confirm this. Pollen analysis shows that the grassland, specifically meadow,

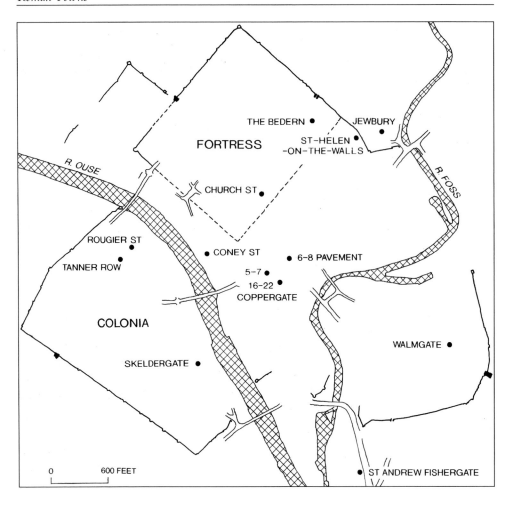

83   York; location of the sites mentioned in chaps 9, 10 and 11. The walls are mostly medieval and later, but they follow the line of the Roman Fortress and Colonia in part

was widespread with no nearby woodland or scrub. So all this indicates that there had been clearance and the establishment of pasture, probably for cattle and horses rather than sheep, with meadow which was being maintained when the Romans arrived. The paucity of archaeological evidence prior to the Roman settlement does not mean a lack of activity; indeed the soil and biology explicitly show a long and sustained human presence, but for the narrow function of stock management.

For the Romans the site was a natural one for a fortress. There was established grassland uncluttered by settlement or trees; it was a low plateau between two rivers; it was on a main routeway between the north and south of eastern Britannia; and it was adjacent to a navigable river with the advantages of tidal-assisted navigation for 76 miles from the estuary, and with access to the sea and the Continent. They came to the area in AD 71 when they began their building of the legionary fortress between the two rivers. The land on the opposite bank of the River Ouse to the south-west, at the foot and on top of a terrace, was also settled in the late first century as a civilian area and by AD 237 had been granted status as a colonia. However, for several decades before that title was granted the area was a vigorous trading settlement, a garrison town with a large civilian population with a high level of economic activity and complexity, as suggested, for example, by the animal bones. Once again, as with other monument types — causewayed camps, mines, hillforts and oppida — formality of physical structure, or charter in the case of the York colonia, was foreshadowed from within the settlement in terms of meaning, status or function.

There is a colossal amount of data from this small town, mostly from small places within it, and each of which is special. The insects and the plants point up the interplay of the physical architecture, the biology and what people were doing. There are also large collections of animal bones. The larger bones are mostly of domesticated animals and are therefore generally relevant to husbandry practices, marketing policy, diet and other aspects of the economy. More specifically, they tell us about practices of slaughter and butchery and how the places where the bones ended up were used.

The Fortress

At the Bedern within the fortress, a mid-second-century timber-lined well had been backfilled by the early to mid-third century. It contained puparia of ten species of fly, indicating that it had been left open long enough to allow these insects to breed in the foul matter; and it contained freshwater and land snails which may have been living in the well. There was human food waste like oyster and mussel shells, bones of cattle, sheep, pig, freshwater fish and a sea fish of tropical waters. Dog bones from an animal with a relatively short muzzle and short legs suggest a pet rather than a hound. Food and other useful plants include some imports like grape, olive, hemp and fig, some which could have been grown locally like walnut, opium poppy, flax, coriander, summer savory and celery, and many which were local and wild and whose status as food is only inferential — examples are a small plum or bullace, sloe, sweet or sour cherry, hazel nut and apple. And there were human faeces as indicated by eggs of human parasitic nematodes — the whipworm (*Trichuris trichiura*) and maw-worm (*Ascaris lumbricoides*) — and wheat/barley bran. There were leaves of box from hedging in ornamental gardens or a ritual context. Altogether, there were over 170 plant taxa and 200 species of beetles and bugs. These indicated the environment around the well to have been waste ground and grassland disturbed by human activity or grazing and with some waterlogged ground. Insects indicate, additionally, spoiled grain, indoor habitats, and dry decaying and foul matter. Other environments from further away were cultivated land, marsh and fen, saltmarsh and heathland. There was also some *Sphagnum* peat.

Generally, it was much more diverse than when the Romans first arrived. Environments were being exploited at a variety of places and distances and through a variety of activities. People brought materials from outside the settlement from heathlands, marshes and peat bogs and took them into their homes, their animal shelters or their places of work. Then they came together, carrying refuse from the butchery, the grain store, the home and the garden and dumped it into the well. Whilst they were there, some of them defecated into it too.

The Colonia

In the colonia (**83**), at Tanner Row, there was 10ft of medieval material which was machined off. The earliest Roman deposits were of the second century AD with timber buildings going into the third century, later to be replaced in stone. Another site, Rougier St, consisted of a stream bed at the base of 23ft of deposits, possibly canalised, a possible riverside wall, and then two successive granaries.

The environment is indicated by more than 350 plant, c500 insect and over 60 other invertebrate taxa. *Period 2 (mid-second century):* Initial use. Aquatic species in ditches, dung beetles and others characteristic of foul matter, and a species found on docks and sorrels (*Rumex*) suggest rough grazing, with the plants themselves — docks, knotgrasses (*Polygonum*) and nitrophile weeds — indicating disturbed ground, cultivation and wet places. Synanthropic insects of buildings, a few grain pests and some woodworm activity; a variety of foodplants. *Period 3 (late second century):* First structural period. Aquatic habitats declined, foul matter was reduced, drier habitats and house fauna became important and there was a significant increase in wood beetles and grain pests. Outdoor insects declined, as through the Roman period generally, but became more diverse. The variety of food plants increased, while parasites and pests became well established. More widely, environments like raised bog and calcareous grassland were exploited. *Period 4 (mid- to late second century):* Silting and dumping sealed previous structures. Grassland taxa and decomposer insects indicate hay and/or horse dung, maybe from stables. *Period 5 (late second century):* Second timber-building range, of oak with a single piece of silver fir (*Abies alba*). No change in biota. *Period 6 (late second to early third century):* Third timber range. Highest proportions of dryland decomposers, house fauna and grain pests for the site. Peat still being brought in but the range of food plants declined. *Period 7 (early to mid-third century):* Stone-buildings. Assemblages similar to before. *Period 8 (fourth century onwards):* Reduction in grain pests; pit fills with human faeces.

Animal bones were mainly from around and between buildings. A small percentage of identified specimens (2-3%) had been gnawed by dogs, and presumably many bones had been totally destroyed by them.

Beef was the main meat in the diet, here and elsewhere in Roman York. Over half the cattle were elderly, presumably valued for dairying and haulage as well. There were no veal calves, but maybe the bones of these were deposited elsewhere. Lamb and pork were important supplements. The sheep were young — 19 out of 60 mandibles being 2-4 months only — meaning a predelication for suckling lamb or ritual, or surplus from flocks kept mainly for dairying. Pigs were mostly young too.

There were various breeds. Cattle were 200-250kg, equivalent to the smallest modern breeds. Eight horn-cores out of around fifty, all from phase 2 of period 5, were typical Celtic shorthorn, very short, tightly curved, and with elliptical basal cross-sections. So there was a mixture of native light cattle and a more heavily horned type. The sheep also included two sizes, mostly a small, probably native, form about the size of a Soay with some of a larger form a bit bigger than a Welsh Mountain ewe. When these larger forms of cattle and sheep were introduced into Britain is unknown, and, although it is tempting to see them as of Roman origin, our previous experiences with clearances and the influence of continental imports of pottery and metalwork in the late prehistoric period

84   *Toad-rush* (Juncus bufonius)

suggests caution. Indeed, they may have originated in the British Isles although the greater proportion in assemblages from south-east England where, too, the large forms are larger than further north, suggests not.

One sample from period 5 contained a preponderance of leg bones of cattle and little else. They were heavily butchered having been split axially and then cut or smashed into smaller pieces. They lacked epiphyses which had been chopped off and also cut into smaller pieces or disposed of elsewhere. This was likely for the extraction of marrow. If it had been for glue or stock then why dispose of the epiphyses, which are an important source of these commodities? From the same period, many samples contained a high proportion of cattle scapulae which were probably boned-out for meat drying; typical features were the removal of the coracoid and spine, probably as a part of the butchery, and the cutting of a rectilinear hole in the blade for hanging up the shoulder to smoke or cure it; the meat was being distributed off the bone. Similar scapulae come from first century deposits within the fortress on the other side of the river. The rapidity with which these leg and scapula deposits accumulated indicates large-scale carcass processing and hence a centralised market-based cash economy.

Additional domestic species were fowl, goose and occasional horse and goat although it is not clear that the last two were eaten. The first British records for the garden dormouse (*Eliomys quercinus*) were from this site, in late second-early third-century deposits. It may have been brought in alive as a delicacy and part of a wider trade in commestibles like oysters, crabs, olives, lentils, figs and grapes; or perhaps it came accidentally with grain, as implied for a further record from South Shields, Tyneside, in granary deposits. Cats and dogs were present. Hunting and fowling added red deer, roe deer, hare, mallard and wild goose, with other bird species indicating water, moorland and farmland; some of the species were winter and some summer visitors, attracted to the floodplains of the Ouse and Derwent.

The house mouse was present as a pest and became increasingly common during the second century, when the black rat (*Rattus rattus*) also became common, with implications for the transmission of plague.

So now we are beginning to see a variety of activities in some detail — husbandry of different breeds, butchery and carcass processing, diet preferences, waste disposal and attitudes to hygiene, and contacts over considerable distances. Now, too, we see these in a specific context, being done in a specific way, and as a result of a specific act: cattle scapulae were removed from the carcass, pierced through the blade and hung as shoulders of meat; they were later filletted, with the removal of the coracoid and spine, and then disposed of. We suspect this was part of a commercial business in Roman York and that it might have been taking place in a part of the town specifically away from the fortress because of attitudes to butchery and hygiene **(p. 123)**. If we could identify the contexts a bit more closely we might see localities in action.

At Skeldergate, also in the colonia, **(83)**, there was an oak-lined well, built somewhere between the late second to mid-third centuries and continuing in use into the late fourth century when it was filled in. There were leather shoes and a bucket made of silver fir (*Abies alba*). Here, too, was the first discovery of several black rats from a Roman context in England and the first record of hemp (*Cannabis sativa*). Many insects were in the well naturally but most of the material is from backfilling.

The large animals were mainly cattle, >70%, mostly mature, and mostly of body parts like horncores, mandibles, scapulae and pelvic fragments indicative of debris from slaughter and initial butchery. The horns had been chopped from the skull indicating use of horn. The jaws had been chopped from the head by a blow into the open mouth probably to extract the tongue, as shown by the way in which the horizontal and vertical parts of the mandibles had been separated. Judging by the paucity of fly puparia and beetles indicative of rotting matter (in contrast to the Bedern well) it seems that the bones were deposited straight after slaughter, which thus took place close by. The bones of sheep, pig and a dog, in contrast, were from domestic waste. One dog was c43.7cm at the shoulder, which is whippet size, and had a long snout **(45)**; a larger dog was represented by an ulna.

The plant remains were from freshwater-marsh and saltmarsh, wasteland and garden including much box, arable and acid peatland, as well as cereals, a few weeds of cultivation, and other food plants. Cereal grain periderm and huge numbers of grain beetles indicate the dumping of spoiled grain. Plants of medicinal value or for poisoning people or animals included hemlock, henbane, deadly nightshade and purging flax, although they may also have been incidental in the background waste land. The insects suggest, in addition, water edges, rotting matter and dung, stored grain, dead wood especially woodworm, and buildings. But the area around the well had been kept clean.

Roman York, general

The establishment and development of the Roman town and fortress entailed the creation of new niches and locales. They included substantial timber buildings, massive stone sewers and formal gardens. There were new plants and animals, some from the British Isles like coastal shellfish and seabirds and some from abroad like olives, dormice and rats. Market-based cash economies were in existence, too, in the form of business in bone and horn products and probably others like metal-work, jewellery and prostitution. But there was also a different sort of structure in that there was a greater range of more extreme niches than anything before; many of the niches were small and closely packed over a large area; they were often short-lived; and all of this was in association with an increasingly dense and diverse human population, in terms of race, kinship and ideas. Previously, in say woodland, or a human settlement, there had been some of these components like ephemerality, small niche size, or extremeness, but there had never been the whole association of characteristics seen in Roman York.

The river, for example, was clean. It did not flood, being lower than it is today by more than 3ft, and it was not brackish. Saltmarsh plants from Roman deposits are thought to have been brought in as ballast, in salt, or herbivore guts in view of the total absence of insect and mollusc species of brackish water or saline influence. There were marsh and other water-edge environments but no reedswamp, suggesting the river was partially canalised and the distinction between water and land kept sharp artificially; we have already noted the evidence for revetment at Rougier St **(p. 120)**. Cattle grazing for which there is abundant evidence in the form of nitrophilous weeds, like nettle (*Urtica dioica*) and goosefoots (*Chenopodium* spp.), would have had the same effect **(p. 23)**.

There were also sharp contrasts in sanitary conditions. Generally, surface-laid deposits are rarely richly organic. Even the wells at Skeldergate and the Bedern and a sewer at Church Street had a relatively low organic content. Deposits are lacking in insect species which like plants of nitrogen- and phosphate-rich soils. This all suggests a Roman environment of well-drained soils, grassland or trampled vegetation and awareness and maintenance of cleanliness. In contrast, in the Rougier St and Tanner Row area of the colonia, there was abundant rotting organic matter during the late second century. The dumping of fresh bones of food animals around and between the buildings created disgusting conditions especially as there were human faeces, raw hay and/or horse dung too. Rats and mice add to this dirtier side of York. It may be a contrast between an unclean service area within the colonia and the cleanliness of the military area of the fortress, although the clean well at Skeldergate is also outside the fortress and the dirty one at the Bedern within it. These accumulations ceased in the late second-early third century with the third timber range and especially in the mid-third century with the change from wooden to stone buildings and the beginnings of the colonia.

There were internal and external parasites of humans and animals and there were pests and vermin. These included human hookworms (*Trichuris trichiura*) and maw-worms (*Ascaris lumbricoides*), human flea (*Pulex irritans*), dog flea (*Cenocephalides canis*), the rat flea (*Nosopsyllus*), human lice (*Pediculus humanus*), house fly (*Musca domestica*), black rats (*Rattus rattus*) and house mice (*Mus domesticus*). There were infestations of the timber of buildings, most of which was oak, with some ash, by woodworm (*Anobium punctatum*) and the powder-post beetle (*Lyctus linearis*). The insides of relatively unclean wooden buildings, including stables, were specific habitats for insects, with damp timber and wattle, moulds and detritus in roofs and walls, plant debris on floors, and the humans themselves.

Stored products were an added dimension, especially cereal grain. Generally in south-east England, spelt wheat (*Triticum spelta*) was the predominant cereal in Roman times; barley (*Hordeum distichum*) was more commonly used for animal fodder and brewing and rye (*Sativa/Secale cereale*) may also have been used for brewing; oats (*Avena sativa*) and brome (*Bromus* or *Zerna*) may have been fortuitous inclusions or weeds but could have been eaten. At York, cereals were bread/club wheat, other hexaploid wheats (probably *Triticum spelta*), six-row barley (*Hordeum distichum*), cultivated oats (*Avena fatua/A. sativa*) and wheat/rye (*Triticum/Sativa*), mainly preserved as periderm, or bran. Roman deposits generally in the city, as in Carlisle, are rich in insects of stored products.

There are two known sites of granaries. At Rougier St, there was a substantial deposit of grain (but no building remains) of the late second century from a store destroyed by fire, mainly spelt (88%), with bread/club wheat or a compact form of spelt (1%), barley at least some of which with distinctively twisted grains was probably six-row barley (11%), oats (0.5%) and a few grains of brome. This was succeeded by a granary (beetle evidence) founded on gritstone pillars to keep the floor dry and above the reach of rats and mice but there was no grain. This site, although some 70yds from the River Ouse today, may have been on the waterfront in the Roman period. At Coney Street on the other side of the river and strategically placed between it and the fortress there was a granary of the first-early second century. The earliest deposit contained no grain, but with 99% of the beetles being grain pest species, mainly the saw-toothed grain beetle (*Oryzaephilus surinamensis*), the rust-red grain beetle (*Cryptolestes ferrugineus*), the grain weevil (*Sitophilus granarius*) and the small-eyed flour beetle (*Paloris ratzeburgi*), with several others in lesser abundance, it is obviously a granary and a severely infested one. These beetles seem to be able to establish colonies from a single impregnated female without any problems arising from inbreeding — an extreme adaptation to an extreme niche. The severity of the Coney Street infestation would have been smelt from the outside and would have been a serious source of contamination: people probably avoided it. It may have led to the deliberate destruction of the store buildings, the remains of which were sealed before a second store was constructed. This contained a large grain deposit, with spelt (54.8/61.0%), barley (23.2/25.0%), rye (9.4/17.8%), brome (6.6/7.6%) and oats (3.6/5.6%) (the percentage ranges are based on several separate counts). Much of the grain in both stores had sprouted indicating another storage problem as well as the insect pests, and recalling the spoiled grain in the Skeldergate well **(p. 122)**. But the granaries of the fortress have never been found, although they are likely to have been just inside one of the gates as is usual practice, presumbly for practicality and as an indication of status.

Indirect evidence of cereal growing is seen in the cornfield weeds **(p. 100)**, especially corncockle (*Agrostemma githago*), wild radish or runch (*Raphanus raphanistrum*), black bindweed (*Bilderdykia convolvulus*) and wild oats (*Avena fatua*) which came into the settlements with the grain, and weed floras seem to have increased dramatically in the Roman period generally.

As well as the parasites, pests and vermin and the cereals and their weeds, a lot of other plants, animals and materials were brought into the settlements from various distances. There was clearly a wide range of contacts and it is likely that there were more of these over greater distances than in prehistory. This increased the opportunities for communication between people in the Eboracum settlements and those elsewhere - locally, further away at the coast and in the hills and valleys, and more remotely in the south of England and abroad. Through these there was an increasing awareness of geography and time, not so much through movements of people, although this was a part of it, but more through conversations about places far away and what came from them.

For example, fragments of raised-bog peat and animals and plants from this environment occur in several contexts, probably brought in for fuel. Plants include *Sphagnum*, mainly *S. imbricatum*, heather (*Calluna vulgaris*), cross-leaved heath (*Erica tetralix*), bog rosemary (*Andromeda polifolia*) and cotton grass (*Eriophorum vaginatum*). Heather may have been brought in on turves or separately from heathland. Some of the mosses, like *Sphagnum*, may have been brought in for bottom-wiping. Some plants and insects, again from the colonia and the Bedern well, were from various types of grassland — of waterside, wet meadow or pasture and calcareous — but it is not possible to determine whether these got in as raw hay or in the digestive tracts of animals that grazed on the pastures, likely horses in view of some of the associated insects. Other plants were for ornament or ritual like box (*Buxus sempervirens*), grown in gardens but also placed in Roman burials. Poppies and various herbs were grown, as was Scots pine (*Pinus sylvestris*) and the stone pine (*Pinus pinea*), the last used as altar fuel. But there was no yew. In addition to the grain, many other food plants were domestic ones. Some of these were imported like olives (*Olea europaea*); others perhaps grew in southern England, like lentils (*Lens culinaris*); some could have grown locally in sheltered places, like grape (*Vitis vinifera*), black mulberry (*Morus nigra*) and fig (*Ficus carica*); and some could definitely have been of local origin, like walnut (*Juglans regia*), flax (*Linum usitatissimum*), broad bean or horse bean (*Vicia faba*) and hemp (*Cannabis sativa*). Another group were wild and only possibly used for food, including a small plum or bullace (*Prunus domestica* ssp. *institia*), sloe (*Prunus spinosa*), sweet or sour cherry (*Prunus* section *Cerasus*), apple (*Malus sylvestris*), hazel nut (*Corylus avellana*), wild strawberry (*Fragaria vesca*), coriander (*Coriandrum sativum*), summer savory (*Satureja hortensis*), celery (*Apium graveolens*), wild carrot (*Daucus carota*), opium poppy (*Papaver somniferum*), blackberry (*Rubus fruticosus* agg.), dewberry (*Rubus caesius*), raspberry (*Rubus idaeus*), elderberry (*Sambucus nigra*), bilberry (*Vaccinium* sp.), rue (*Ruta graveolens*) and possibly dill (*Anethum graveolens*).

The domestic animals were various breeds and sizes of cattle and sheep, as well as horses, pigs, goats, garden dormice (*Eliomys quercinus*), domestic fowl and goose. There were two breeds of dogs, one with a long muzzle possibly for hunting, another with a shorter muzzle and shorter legs possibly kept as pets. There were cats may be for pets and keeping down mice. Game was wild boar, hare (*Lepus europaeus*), roe and red deer, various birds, at least a dozen species of freshwater and estuarine fish and a few sea fish — herring and an unidentified sparrid. Food invertebrates included sea crabs (*Cancer pagurus*) and shellfish, oysters (*Ostrea edulis*) and mussels (*Mytilus edulis*).

Specialisation

In prehistory, there had probably been a complete lay knowledge of all the processes of procuring the materials for living, as Peter Dickens has described in his book, *Reconstructing nature*. (The probable exception is metal-working.) Butchery, for example, as a discrete event did not exist. In one direction there was an ongoing business of dealing with the various parts of an animal from its death to its complete disappearance. In the other direction, butchery was envisioned way back, in the various uses of the animals, in their rearing, and further back in the husbandry of particular breeds. Any distinction between meat as the primary product and marrow, milk, skins and traction as secondary ones is, in this light, futile. Equally, how a process took place and what it resulted in were as much related to the expressive order as to perceptions of an end result — or, more realistically, successive end results. The precise course of events was never predictable; subtle changes were always going on.

However, these two aspects of prehistoric life — complete and individual lay knowledge and, at the same time, unpredictability — were starting to be eroded in these early towns. There was still contact with the countryside, for example in the practices of gardening and even cereal cultivation and the contacts with animal products for manuring that these entailed. But there were the beginnings of husbandry practices like the rearing of particular breeds which were specifically rural business. And there were the beginnings of a money-based marketing economy, large-scale carcass processing and wholesale redistribution which were specifically urban business. Obviously there was a relationship between town and country, with organised contacts and supplies from surrounding farms, but knowledge of the whole histories between these different areas no longer belonged to any one individual. The combination of many small and many extreme niches and a concentration of people who depended on them entailed a total focusing on specific activities — looking after granaries, cleaning out sewers or processing horn. And, the influx of unfamiliar materials which needed processing and in ways which needed to be learnt, together with the diversity of people of unfamiliar appearances, races and homelands, meant that more formality was needed. One could now begin to talk of *husbandry* and see it as a separate process from *butchery*, the *extraction* of marrow or the *disposal* of bone debris. This is really what is meant by specialisation — doing something with more formality, less expression, and less lay knowledge of the entire complexity of events.

10 Dark earth and Anglian and Anglo-Scandinavian York

Dark earth

The period towards the end of Roman rule in Britain and the century or so subsequently — really the late fourth and the fifth centuries AD — is sometimes seen as a period when towns were deserted. In some towns it is marked by a thick deposit of dark loam called 'dark earth', the colour being due to charcoal and organic matter. 'There was no functional survival of Roman urbanisation in Britain. Excavations at London, Canterbury, Gloucester and Winchester show a break in soil type that makes it most unlikely that any substantial population existed there between AD 450 and 600' (D Nicholas 1997, *The growth of the medieval city*).

Much of the recent work on dark earth has been done by Richard Macphail, largely through micromorphology. In Southwark and London, sites between the second-fourth and tenth centuries are represented by one uniform layer, up to 6.5ft thick, so dark earth can have a longer duration than just the immediate two centuries following Roman collapse, although this is a composite picture from several sites. In some cases it began to form in the third century as a response to urban decline and a reduction in the area settled. However, this idea has received a knock recently from Roman Lincoln where organised and substantial beef storage and provisioning, systematic rubbish disposal, centralised grain storage in heated buildings as indicated by the long-term survival of cockroaches, and altogether disciplined urban organisation existed from the early third to the late fourth centuries. At Worcester, the dark earth overlies late Roman levels and is in turn overlain by the rampart of the Saxon burh, although in one area late Roman inhumations cut through the dark earth.

Macphail interprets the deposit variously. A crucial common theme is that biological processes of soil formation homogenise and mask previously heterogeneous materials. Casts of earthworms and enchytraeid worms (wireworms) are common and so are the calcareous granules of these animals and molluscs. Sometimes there was a succession, with earthworm casts being thoroughly reworked by enchytraeids and then the whole fabric being further modified by other soil processes under grassland. The modification of materials from collapsed or demolished buildings is an important source. Fragments of slag, building debris, plaster and mortar are abundant often in a matrix of fine charcoal and humified organic matter. Occasional stone buildings 'floating' in dark earth point up these processes of homogenisation. 'Analogues from bombed sites in Berlin and London indicate that fauna and flora in abandoned urban areas can transform a variety of urban deposits into homogeneous dark earth.'

At the macro-scale, a variety of human processes was involved, and these were often what we today might consider as of a non-urban type — like animal penning and garden cultivation. Sometimes more than one process occurred sequentially. This seems to have been the case at Southwark where mid-second century buildings were destroyed and overlain by dark earth containing third-fourth century pottery. Spreading of rubbish continued the build up into as late as the end of the fourth century, and previously built-up areas were given over to market gardening towards the end of the Roman period. Dark earth continued to accumulate into medieval and post-medieval times. At Deansway, Worcester, late-Roman midden material and burned stable manure was indistinguishable from overlying dark earth formed under grassland. In London, at Whittington Ave., first century Roman horticulture reworked a burned-down timber and clay building, while agriculture at Culver St, Colchester, transformed debris from the Boudiccan revolt into a cultivation soil. Sometimes, overlying medieval garden soil is superficially indistinguishable from dark earth, and the spreading of materials can be contributory in creating and accentuating its uniformity. Dark earth represents a greater variability of human activity than is suggested by its uniformity in the field.

One is tempted to see the dark earth as a definitive episode in urban history because of its distinctive characters and widespread distribution. However, much urban archaeology like the construction and destruction of buildings, levelling with materials and the digging of pits, reflects changes which were often of short duration. Many of the activities reflected in pits and wells and between houses in Roman York were the result of rapid, even individual, dumpings **(p. 123)**. In contrast, the areas where everyday life goes on, like the actual areas of house floors and street surfaces, are reflected poorly in the stratigraphy because they were kept clean. It is only when people were doing something that allowed soil and deposits to accumulate gradually while the activity was still going on that we get deposits which reflect the more continuous duration of life. This seems to be what was occurring with the dark earth. There does not need to have been a period of desertion for it to have formed; it took place contemporaneously with the presence and activities of people.

Crucially, too, dark earth reflects a more general feature of towns, namely the introduction of materials from the rural hinterland, like building materials, stock, manure, fodder and bedding, which were then not recycled like they are in the countryside but allowed to accumulate. This is a further reflection of the specialised activities that go on in towns, both generally **(p. 126)** and as a result of the constricted physical geography of buildings and the partitioned tenurial geography of land. Thus a lot of human effort inadvertently went into raising levels of the land. Rivers provide one outlet, and the site of Fishergate **(83)** next to the River Foss in York is remarkably clean of bones because of this. There was also a food web based on scavenging animal communities, like red kites and white-tailed eagles as described by J Bond & T O'Connor for York, which grew up in denser populations than in the countryside because of the continuous supply of food. But the birds were limited more by nesting sites and human intervention than by food, and they still could not get rid of mineral matter. So the surface level rose. In the countryside, in contrast, where there was more space, less intensive occupation and a greater knowledge and application of the way life worked, waste materials were naturally recycled or dumped in quarries, at the foot of steep ground or along boundaries.

York between the Romans and the Vikings

At York there is no good evidence for extensive dark earth, although some of the later ninth century pitfills at Coppergate (**85**) resemble it. In some areas, including Coppergate, homogeneous loams formed in the fifth to the mid-ninth centuries during disuse. They may be alluvial, but their precise origin is quite unclear. According to Richard Hall, York in the fifth and sixth centuries is obscure, but it had a church by AD 627 and King Edwin of Deira probably had a palace there. By the mid-seventh century the Roman defences were being rebuilt and there was a mint. There is an eighth-century helmet from a wood-lined shaft only 30ft from the Coppergate site.

Eoforwic, an Anglian trading station

At Fishergate in the south of the city on land to the east of the River Foss (**83**) there was an Anglian trading settlement or wic, Eoforwic. This was established in the very late seventh century and became deserted around AD 850 or immediately before the Viking capture of York in AD 866. Ditches and pits cut through a Roman ploughsoil, immediately above which was the Anglian soil. There was no intervening dark earth, although there was an extensive layer of soil of uniform thickness with ash, charcoal and bone fragments between two Anglian horizons, which formed when the area was deliberately levelled.

The suggestion that this site was a wic is based on its siting at the confluence of the Rivers Ouse and Foss and on finds of imported pottery from northern France or Belgium, Frisian coins, glass vessels and lava querns. The animal bones, too, are consistent with the idea of a trading station. Thus the age at death of the domesticated animals is not what one would expect in a self-sufficient producer community, that is with a range of ages, indicative of many different usages, and with primary and secondary butchery as parts of a continuous process being done in the same place. Nor is it what occurs in a consumer town where meat is traded directly with producers, where there is specialisation on certain products but at the same time a broad subsistence base, and with wholesale and retail butchery as distinct entities. Rather there was a narrow range of diet and an especial impoverishment in the animals that are most suited to being kept in towns like pigs, hens and geese or directly obtained there like fish from the rivers. The pigs that were present were age-selected and possibly brought in as dressed carcasses. There were also few wild birds in comparison to urban sites. All this supports central provisioning of the settlement for its subsistence needs by a controlling authority. Pine martens were being skinned and there was beaver.

Skeldergate

In the area of Skeldergate (**83**), major reorganisation took place in the tenth century in later Anglian or Anglo-Scandinavian times, with the establishment of several buildings, over the filled-in Roman well (**p. 122**). Bones came from tenth-century occupation associated with a succession of timber buildings. Many of the bones had been gnawed by dogs. Cattle were predominant. One sample, with high frequencies of heads, pelves and scapulae, indicated secondary butchery waste; another, with a higher frequency of uppper limb bones, kitchen debris. But it is not possible to translate this into a rigid division of

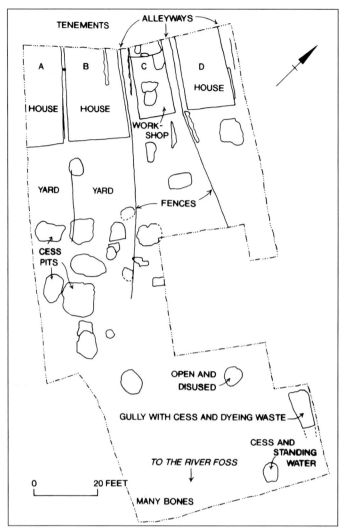

85   16-22 Coppergate, tenements A to D, period 4B. (Based on Kenward & Hall 1995)

slaughter, butchery and consumption in the tenth-century city as whole. Indeed there are alternative interpretations which see these assemblages as mixed or as representing the entire sequence from slaughter to consumption. All the livestock were slaughtered at an age for prime meat; milk, wool and traction were of lesser importance.

There were some nice details of butchery. Cattle heads were removed from the carcass by a blow through the axis or third cervical vertebra. The carcasses had been chopped transversely, as in the production of fore-rib or T-bone cuts, and not lengthwise as in the production of sides. Limb bones had been chopped into small pieces and mostly lengthwise to extract marrow or reduce the size for stock boiling, as too had tarsals (hind ankle bones) and scapulae. There had clearly been considerable use made of the bones themselves. Horse bones had been similarly treated so horse meat too may have been eaten. A sheep skull had been chopped sagittally, probably to remove the brain, and the horns had been cut off.

Anglo-Scandinavian York

The depths of deposits are staggering. There are 30ft of deposits in the Coppergate area, although not all of it Anglo-Scandinavian. In the area of the Minster it is over 34ft from the modern surface down to the Roman one. It gives you some idea to go into the undercroft of the Gothic Cathedral which itself is 14ft below the modern streets, and totally encloses an earlier Norman Cathedral, and look down through an opening in the floor to the north-west corner of the Roman headquarters, 20ft further down still. This is all as high as a two storey house.

6-8 Pavement and 5-7 Coppergate

Vikings took over York in AD 866 and began to settle there in 876. An area between the two rivers centred on Coppergate (**83**) is rich in their remains, and the following account is based on the report by Alan Hall and his colleagues in the York Environmental Archaeological Unit.

The settlement consisted of tenements which were on ground sloping down to the Foss, and although influenced by high water-tables the area was not flooded during the Anglo-Scandinavian settlement. The sequence spans the late ninth-late tenth centuries (C-14 and pottery), with dendrochronology of timbers indicating felling dates of AD 940-50, 970 and 990. There was up to 20ft of organic peaty loams varying from strongly humified to almost raw plant tissue and other organic debris with no inorganic content at all; grass (?hay) and straw, brought to the buildings for thatch and bedding, and sometimes occurring in animal dung, and heather are important components. Within this matrix is a succession of as many as eleven phases of post, stake-and-wattle buildings with internal floors of, variously, beaten earth, mortar or planks, hearths and rubbish. 5-7 Coppergate consisted of rich organic deposits with horizontal wattle and a stake-and-wattle alignment, and of Anglo-Scandinavian to Norman date.

The plant and animal remains were mostly preserved because of waterlogging, and this means that this was present right from the start. Macroscopic plant remains are mainly from disturbed habitats such as waste ground and arable with the regular occurrence of species indicative of nitrogen and phosphate-rich soils, and some influence of aquatic habitats. Hop (*Humulus lupulus*) and pea (*Pisum sativum*) can be added to the lists of species of economic importance not present in Roman times. The major timbers were of oak, with ash and alder for more slender ones, hazel, alder, willow and birch for brushwood and wattle, and pine for planks. The beetles are mostly synanthropes typical of decaying matter. There are wood-boring beetles, a very few grain beetles (possibly residual from Roman deposits), and species of water, water-edges and open ground.

Similar deposits, although especially deep in the Coppergate/Pavement area, occur widely in York. How did they form? Common factors may be long-lived settlement, short-lived buildings and a large organic input. Once this kind of waterlogged environment had been established, timbers of buildings would have been susceptible to decay at ground level, maybe as quickly as in ten years as suggested by experiments with oak posts, and so the buildings would have been frequently replaced. Rotting matter was present *in situ* as shown by the super-abundance of some species of insect, the presence of pale and congenitally mutilated individuals which could not have dispersed actively, and the abundance of blind and flightless species and fly puparia, all foul-rotters and compost-dwellers. Some of the deposits formed outside and were moist and foul. Others formed indoors on floors, although it is unlikely that people actually lived on this sort of surface. Much more likely is that they accumulated in buildings not being used all the time, or at the edges of buildings, in enclosed middens, or in the narrow spaces between the buildings where rubbish was dumped.

16-22 Coppergate

This is the site of the main Viking excavation (**83, 85, 86**) and where there is now the Jorvik Centre with its reconstructed Viking buildings and life. The period of interest is from the mid-ninth century, when occupation is first recorded after apparent desertion since the late fourth century, to the mid-eleventh century, after which buildings no longer survive. The following account is from Richard Hall's book on *Viking Age York* and the work on the plants, insects and bones by Alan Hall, Harry Kenward and Terry O'Connor, with my own ideas.

The earliest evidence for Anglo-Scandinavian occupation, cAD 870-900 (period 3), was open-air, comprising hearth, oven or kiln bases and huge pits over 12ft deep. At least one of the pits had a wickerwork lining, the careful construction belying its foul purpose of waste disposal from domestic, byre and industrial sources, with even a few human bones. Many of the animal bones showed signs of gnawing by dogs and some by cats, so a lot of rubbish had been lying around before being put into the pits.

As with the Bedern Roman well (**p. 119**) a variety of activites and distances from the pits are reflected in the deposits, and there was subtle variation in what was being deposited from layer to layer and in the decomposition of the fills. Some contained moist nutrient-rich material like dung and mud, human faeces and branching mosses and wool, so people were likely defecating straight into the pits. From houses nearby, floor sweepings already contained materials from a variety of distances before they were brought to the pits, comprising hay, straw, bracken, heather and reeds, as well as human fleas and lice. Bones indicated beef and dairy products as mainstays of the human diet, used litter showed that the cattle byres were close by, and saltmarsh plants from the dung suggested that the animals were pastured along estuaries and the coast (**p. 123**). There were dye plants and teasels so dyeing and textile-working was taking place nearby as well. There were also differences between pits and groups of pits. Some were filled quickly and sealed, others left open, attracting annoying and disease-carrying flies. Walking through the area at any one time was an experience in different sorts of smells and, if you prodded the material or fell in, of textures and consistencies.

This is a segment of the early Viking settlement. It was an area of waste ground of disturbed nutrient-rich soils with nitrophile weeds, nettles and a rooted elder. Plants of seasonally wet paths, like the toad-rush (*Juncus bufonius*) (**84**), added to the diversity. It was in part an industrial area maybe for glassworking in the open air, and in part for the disposal of household rubbish. It was stinking and dangerous. But it was still likely a part of some small child's universe and her dog's.

In c930/935-975 (period 4B), four tenements with boundaries going towards the

86   *16-22Coppergate,*
      tenements A to D.
      General plan of periods
      4B and 5B.
      Open areas and
      continuous lines =
      pits and walls of 4B;
      stippled and cross
      hatched = pits,
      drains and walls of
      5B;
      black = areas usedin
      both periods.
      (Based on Kenward
      & Hall 1995)

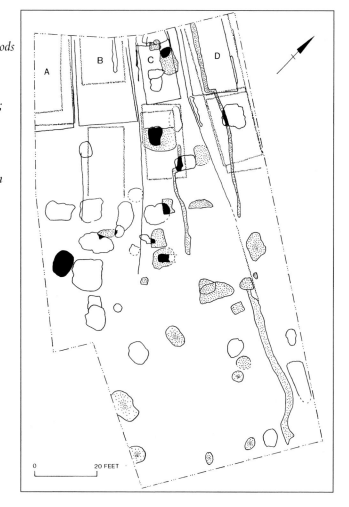

River Foss (**85**) were constructed on top of the infilled pits of period 3. Presumably they represent the same sort of settlement as period 3, in which case it was being moved around or expanded. The houses were single-storey, rectangular and of post-and-wattle without daub (although there is daub in some pits). One end fronted Coppergate (if it existed then), but the position of any front doors is unknown, while the other opened onto a yard. The floors were of compacted loam and earth, levelled material dug out of pits and from earlier buildings. The actual floors on which people lived were kept clean and dry, or had litter of straw, hay and heather that was rarely foul and was devoid of animal and human dung, although there were some puparia of flies (*Musca domestica* and *Stomoxys calcitrans*). There were no faeces, and human internal worms were rare. There was ash dispersed from hearths, food debris like hazel-nut shells, and some harmless debris from craft processes. Ectoparasites included human fleas (*Pulex irritans*) and lice (*Pediculus humanus*). Much of this material was probably piled up under wall benches of which there were some structural remains. There were substantial hearths in three of the tenements (the one in tenement A had probably been destroyed), one stone-lined, one with Roman tiles and one with timber beam surrounds. These suggest that the buildings were dwellings, and this is supported by the abundant human lice which indicate grooming and by the range of food plants especially flavourings. There was no separate space for animals or even insect evidence for their presence.

The buildings were also used as workshops. There was metal-working of iron, copper alloy, lead alloy, silver and gold, with many crucibles. Textile working, or at least wool cleaning, is indicated by sheep keds and lice (*Damalinia ovis*), and flax was processed. Dye plants, like dyer's greenwood, madder (*Rubia tinctorum*) and clubmoss are well represented, and there were bees and beeswax. Tenement C may have been a workshop specifically as the building was smaller than the others, but with a bigger yard (**85**), and there were open pits inside with dyeing waste, abundant remains of bees and, in one, dung or stable/byre cleanings. But there were no human faeces.

Surface deposits in the alleys between the buildings, less than 3ft wide, were not especially moist and foul, although some were. There were nettles, grass and toad-rush growing between houses B and C where there was also a wattle path and the bony core of a brown bear claw.

The backyards were used for dumping all sorts of materials although there were no discrete middens. Materials range from house floor-sweepings, cornfield weeds from straw or threshing debris, to occasional human faeces with worms, food plants and dyeing waste. Beyond the limit of the tenement divisions, annual weeds were common and there was one area of abundant animal-bone debris, but there was no foul matter. There were many pits in the backyards, some huge, wicker-lined and over 10ft deep, containing ample human faeces, sometimes as discrete turds, sometimes unconsolidated, with large numbers of parasite worm eggs and bran as well as branching mosses and woollen yarn. Fly puparia were abundant. These pits were clearly for cess, at least at some periods. There was also a range of other materials from domestic waste and faeces, like bracket fungi, charred bread, dog-dirt, feathers, daub, sloe stones and eel and herring vertebrae.

In general, occupation was intensive, rubbish accumulating rapidly in and around the buildings and being disposed of in the backyards. But in spite of the organic nature of the deposits and impression of squalor, the pits were used specifically for cess, the yards were used for general dumping and were not especially noisesome, the alleyways had grass and other plants growing in them, and the house floors and interiors were kept clean. The houses were sometimes destroyed by fire or rotted and were dismantled. They were repaired or rebuilt often. The houses and fences which are recorded are presumably a late stage in the sequence although some remains of earlier buildings on the same places were found.

In 973, as shown by dendrochronology, there was a major reconstruction (period 5B), although with the same four tenements being maintained. There were now two ranks of buildings, front and back (**86**), and they differed in structure, significantly in having sunken semi-basement floors, 6ft below the surface and in being plank-built. They were dug out of 4B material which was also used as levelling material, thus creating havoc with the stratigraphy. The functional implications of this change of style is that the buildings were stronger and supported an upper storey where the hearths were likely to have been. There was variation in plan and building style but the contemporaneous reorganisation of the four tenements suggests to Richard Hall a single ownership. Metalworking continued and there were new trades. The same kind of activities in relation to rubbish accumulation and disposal seem to have gone on as for the earlier period 4B. There was a concentration of honey bees between buildings C and D.

In both periods, the tenements were long, presumably going from a street at the front down to the river at the back. Visitors to the houses may have entered from the front of each house, or down the alleys between them where they were not too narrow and through the back door. The central feature of the interiors was the hearth each with its different construction. People sat on benches along the sides of the buildings or around the hearth and there were lamps. Their valuables and other belongings were kept in locked chests which could also have been seats. They cooked, talked, groomed and slept inside, and probably in well-defined areas. They disposed of rubbish outside in the yard and in pits and they defecated into the pits too. Only one pit was probably open at a time, although a few towards the far end of the tenements were open more permanently (**85**), and they were probably cordoned off against children, drunkards and animals. There do not seem to have been middens although these may have been further down towards the Foss where material could have been collected by boat and taken to the fields. There was probably farmland a few hundred yards up the Foss, and contact with local farmers could have been profitable. Crafting took place inside and outside in the yard, again probably in particular areas.

Were they farmers too? The animal bones help to answer this. Butchery of cattle was done on the settlement with no evidence of a distinction between primary and secondary butchery. Unlike in the Roman colonia, there were no specialised meat retailers. The pattern of age at death suggests cattle for meat but also for haulage and dairy - with no specialistion in any one area. This is what might be expected with small independent farms, with most animals being slaughtered after two-and-a-half years old and very few young calves (below 12 months). Haulage by cattle is indicated by arthropathy in the lower-limb and hip bones, and there is evidence of horn-yokeing in one eburnated neck vertebra. Among the cattle, high frequencies of possibly congenital abnormalities suggest a small gene-pool and thus the livestock populations of small farming communities. Although size was fairly constant and similar to the smallest multi-purpose breeds of recent times, there was considerable variation in horncore form suggesting a degree of diversity again consistent with the idea of many individual small-scale farms. The same conclusions apply to the sheep, with the animals being used for a variety of purposes and different kinds of wool. So it is possible that the same families were involved in farming and small-scale crafts and industry, although some animals may still have had to have been brought from considerable distances to the town.

There may have been some pig-breeding actually on the site in the yards of some of the tenements, since bones of foetal and perinatal animals were found, implying at least the presence of farrowing sows. One pit in tenement B in period 4B contained pig faeces and nematode eggs. Horse and goat were probably kept for various purposes and formed a minor part of the diet. Four cats were skinned. Dogs ranged in size from smaller than fox to as large as wolf, with most being collie-size. Domestic fowl and goose, and their eggs, were abundant. There were black rats and house mice and a few other small mammals.

Many of these animals would have done a lot of cleaning up in the yards and around the buildings as well as providing prey for the cats.

There was some hunting of wild boar, hare, red deer (although mostly shed antlers) and roe deer. There were a few bear phalanges, probably from skins, a fox and an otter. Three red squirrel foot bones were probably from pelts **(p. 146)**. There were 31 bird species, mostly from wetlands but also from woodland and moorland, with birds of prey, and razorbill and guillemot from coastal cliffs, matching the botanical and insect evidence for use of these habitats. About 35 fish species were mainly of herrings, cod, salmon, pike, carp and eels, and with freshwater, estuarine and salt-water habitats all represented. The eels, especially, probably came from the rivers of the settlement.

Town people knew about and involved themselves in country pratices, even if there were still distinct urban and rural ecologies. This was not just through the building of the houses by the people that lived in them but also the gathering of the raw materials from the countryside and even their management by those same people. Different species were being used for different purposes, thus allowing an articulation between different components of a building (and their uses by different people in the household) with different trajectories of exploitation. There was probably no strong conception of separate parts of a lineal process. With wooden houses, the constant need for maintenance and rebuilding made these associations with the raw materials stronger. Partly this was in the area of practicalities which we can easily understand and which relate to the biophysical surrounds: the building of houses and planning of settlements near to water and other resources, the need for company and, within the house, the whereabouts of places for cooking and sex. But more than this, it was about relationships within the household and the impressions householders gave to the outside world, and these took place through the whole process from woodland management through house construction to the use of individual locales, like different styles of hearths.

This was facilitated by flexibility of movement between different areas and settlements. In the summer or at festivals, people may have moved to other towns to sell their crafts, and quite a number of the buildings in this part of York may have been left for a few months. They may have been used by other people from another town doing the same thing or there may have been exchange with some of the people in nearby farms belonging to the same family. Nadia Seremetakis describes this kind of 'economic and cultural agility' for Inner Mani in southern Greece: 'Most Maniat women pass back and forth between urban and rural socioeconomic and residential settings, code-switching between and within rural and urban cultures . . .' 'In doing so they construct a third cultural continuum neither completely rural nor urban.' More and more we see the same sort of thing in our own Western lives with weekly commuting between urban financial or academic centres and rural villages, which in no way function as they did even 30 years ago.

11 Medieval York

In this chapter we look at some histories of medieval York, and in doing so bring environmental archaeology into a period where it does not often feature significantly. York also allows us to look at cemeteries, again not traditional in the subject, and thus to make the point that environmental archaeology is integral to archaeology as a whole. The following account of two of these is taken from the detailed recording and analysis published in reports of the York Archaeological Trust.

Medieval cemeteries of St Andrew, Fishergate

At Fishergate (**83**), after the Anglian wic, there was a period of about 150-200 years when we do not know what went on. A new settlement was established in the late tenth or early eleventh century and this was followed a few decades later by the beginnings of the use of the area for religious purposes which was to last almost 500 years. There were two successive Christian cemeteries, both associated with churches, thus allowing a complex interplay between the position in the community of the people being buried, the architecture of church and liturgy, and the location of their graves.

The first cemetery (period 4) belonged to a settlement that may have been part of a ribbon suburb along Fishergate. It was established in the mid-eleventh century (period 4b), associated with a wooden church. An exceptionally large grave contained the bones of an individual aged 12-14 yrs that had been wrapped, presumably in a shroud, and buried in an advanced state of decomposition; it was positioned to the east of the church in precise alignment with its long axis. There were twelve males with blade injuries that may all have been battle casualties and all buried at once in one area. The cemetery continued in use into the twelfth century (period 4d), with the church possibly being replaced in stone; there were 5 further battle casualties. In the cemetery as a whole the demographic profile suggested full representation of the community, apart from the slight emphasis on males in the battle casualties. There was a tendency for children to be buried in separate areas, with groups of two or three and a quite distinct cluster of 16 at the far west end. There were 5 double graves, one triple grave, one decapitation and a further 2 with blade injuries. They were in north-south rows but rather irregularly placed. There were 131 in total.

The second cemetery, from 1195 to the sixteenth century (period 6), belonged to a Gilbertine priory. There were successive periods of burial and priory re-structuring until 1538 when the priory was dissolved, and these disturbances are reflected in numerous charnel deposits where loose bones were re-buried.

Location within the claustral complex (relation to the priory buildings), burial trappings, and age and sex associations allowed the identification of different life communities in the cemetery (**87**). Areas for the lay people had varying numbers of males, females and

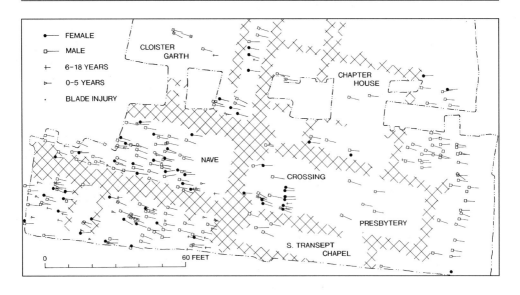

87   *Monastic cemetery (period 6) at St Andrew Fishergate. Walls cross-hatched. (Based on Stroud*
      & Kemp 1993)

sub-adults, with importance being indicated by the proportions of stone coffins (high status), wooden coffins with iron fittings, unbound wooden coffins, and no coffins (low status). The north transept chapel and east cloister alley were the most important areas, where patrons, for example, might have been buried, while the nave and crossing were less important; other areas of lay burial were south of the nave and the cloister garth. But there were still far more males than females in the cemetery to the south of the nave, suggesting a definitive relationship with the monastery with perhaps servants and their families being buried there. Five double graves and close associations of one male and one female and sometimes of a child suggest family groupings, as do associations of specific congenital bone anomalies. There were 10 male burials with blade injuries and one decapitation. These were in areas of lay community burials except for one in the chapter house. Some of the injuries were vicious, cut skulls, pierced pelves and hacked vertebrae, and some of the piercing injuries may have been from arrows. One skull had striation patterns due to defects of the edge of the sword which matched on two of the cut surfaces and which also indicated the direction of the blow. Other areas — the presbytery and north-east of it, the chapter house and around the east end of the church — were used specifically by the monastic community; they contained either all adult males or mostly males with a thin fringe of females, although important lay people like founders, benefactors and their families could have been buried in these areas too. Status here was also indicated by grave contents especially lead alloy chalices and patens suggesting the burial of priests. The eastern burial ground also had a higher proportion of older individuals than elsewhere, suggesting better sanitary conditions and hygiene in the monastery than in the town and this is supported by evidence from monasteries in other parts of England where the organisation and condition of drainage and storage were superior to those in town dwellings generally. A total of 281 burials was recorded.

Taking both cemeteries together, there was considerable uniformity in burial practice, and variations are quite subtle. Of seven types, the vast majority (245 out of 264, burial type 1) were in graves, where these could be recognised, and some in wooden coffins held together with wooden pegs and a few with nails and clench nails. Of the others, 11 were in monolithic or composite stone coffins (type 2), one a re-used Roman sarcophagus; 2 were in graves lined with unused ceramic roof-tiles (type 3); one, a blade-injured and decapitated burial, had cobbles around the skull (type 4); 2 had uninscribed stone slabs at the head (type 5); two, both child burials, were in graves lined with slabs or stones (type 6); and one was in a grave lined with lime (type 7). All the burials were laid on their backs, stretched out, but with different positionings and degrees of flexure of legs and arms, possibly indicating status, age or gender. Again, however, most of the burials (225 out of 270) were in only two of these positions, namely arms at the sides or on the body. All were aligned east-west, heads at the west, except one burial of a decapitation in period 6 with its head to the east.

Medieval Jewish cemetery at Jewbury

The cemetery

The medieval Jewish cemetery is just outside the city walls, where it had to be by custom, on the north-east side in rural land sloping down to the River Foss (**83, 88**). A rectangular area, c2ac (0.8ha), was enclosed by a boundary ditch, and possibly a wall, on three sides, with the river possibly being the fourth. Medieval documents tell us it was owned by the Jews and in use between 1177, at the earliest, and 1290 when the Jews were expelled from England. Initially it was shared by the Jews of Lincoln and possibly Northampton and Stamford. Nearly 500 individuals were excavated and the likely total buried is between 900 and 1060.

The burials were highly uniform, most having been placed in wooden coffins, some of Scots pine, held together with iron nails. A few, 20 out of 441, were of oak with coffin fittings of iron corner brackets and straps, perhaps evidence of grander status although this was generally eschewed by the Jews. Certainly it was in contrast to the much greater diversity in Christian cemeteries as at St Helen-on-the-Walls and Fishergate (**83**). There were also fewer body positions at Jewbury, e.g. only nine different arm positions as against 24 at Fishergate, indicating more care and standardisation. The burials were aligned north-north-east to south-south-west, probably as related to one of the boundaries. The direction of the head was random. There were no grave goods, again in contrast to the Christian cemeteries where there was a smattering.

The cemetery was highly organised (**88**). In Jewish practice, the dead should not be disturbed, and accordingly few graves intercut (12% intercuts with only 1.7% causing damage to a previous burial) except in two areas. This was in contrast to St Helen-on-the-Walls and the Fishergate priory cemetery with 35% and 40% intercuts respectively. Clearly the Jews took more care than the Christians to avoid disturbing the dead, and this is reflected generally in Jewish cemeteries by the absence of charnel pits and randomly scattered bones. Even so, some burials were very close to each other. Where there was intercutting it could have been due to overcrowding, either prior to the

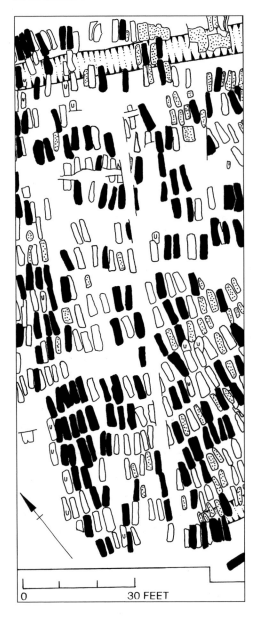

88 *Part of the Jewish burial ground at*
Jewbury.
Black = males;
open = females;
stippled = children;
u = unsexed.
Note early cemetery boundary ditches, at
top and bottom of diagram, overlain by
burials.
(Based on Lilley et al. 1994)

purchase of a cemetery extension in 1230 or during the 1280s towards the end of its use.
As with many Jewish cemeteries, the burials were in rows and regularly spaced. Only five
had markers, and there were no gravestones, although these may have been destroyed after
the expulsion. Several rows were in use at a time and not filled from one end or the other;
it is possible that certain areas in rows were reserved for certain individuals. Associations
of a few individuals in terms of discontinuous skeletal traits, like metopism (presence of a
frontal suture) or epipteric bones, suggest the grouping of relatives. There was also some
clustering of the sexes, especially males who were possibly rabbis and in areas specifically
for them. Children were grouped, as at a Jewish cemetery in Winchester, but as also at

Fishergate and other Christian cemeteries in England. There was a distinct difference between the ordered earlier southern part of the cemetery and the more irregular later northern one.

The population

From the skeletons themselves we can examine demography, physique and pathology. We can also make comparisons with populations from other cemeteries in York, like that of St Helen-on-the-Walls, one of the poorer York parishes (**83**), and from the surrounding countryside, like that from Wharram Percy, a small village population in the Yorkshire wolds, based in part on the synthesis by Don Brothwell. But to make further inferences about, for example, nutrition, growth, health (including psychological health) and working conditions, is tricky because of their complex aetiology. Psychological stress, for example, can influence physiology, physique and genetics. It can cause eating disorders, ovulation to be missed, reduction in fertility and even genetic mutations. And it can lead to death: people retiring early or living in the company of animals live longer than those who do not. But how do we isolate stress and distinguish it from, say, dietary or nutritional influences on, say, stature or longevity?

Demography. The medieval Jewish population of York was estimated as between around 200-360 individuals at any one time. In the cemetery, there were equal numbers of males, females and children, but young children are probably under-represented, as at St Helen-on-the-Walls, judging by comparisons with other medieval cemeteries and post-medieval parish registers, and this suggests a special place for their burial which was not found. In contrast, individuals dying before their mid-teens make up just over a quarter and this is no different from other sites. Distribution of age at death was similar for males and females, the highest number of deaths in both sexes being in the 20-30 age group. This was all similar to St Helen-on-the-Walls, York Minster and pre-monastic Fishergate. There was no difference betweeen male and female death rate, the two sexes being in equal numbers at 35yrs, whereas it is often the case that females die much younger because of childbirth. Thus at St Helen-on-the-Walls, 56% adult females had died by the age of 35 compared with only 36% males. In contrast to other medieval populations, the Jewish community had a surprising number living beyond fifty years, with women, especially, more likely to live into old age than those at St Helen-on-the-Walls. Life expectancies for Jewbury, averaged 24yrs at birth and 23+yrs at 14. Living conditions may have been something to do with this, as suggested for the high proportion of mid-adults in the monastic cemetery at Fishergate, and for York in the fifteenth and sixteenth centuries, where there was higher life expectation in wealthy heirs and aristocrats in comparison with people of six urban York parishes. For the York Jews, however, affluence may be an unwarranted assumption; there was substantial variability in wealth and status across the community and through time, with an especial decline in the last thirty years before the expulsion in 1290.

Physique. Some aspects, like stature, robustness and dental crowding, come through in the living individual; others, like long-bone flattening, may not always be so displayed;

while features such as abnormal thickness and modifications to the internal surface of the skull, as seen in the Jewbury population, or the spinal anomalies in some of the Fishergate skeletons, are even more cryptic and can be revealed only in surgery or after death.

Taking skull measurements first: although a Yorkshire medieval sample as a whole clusters closely, and with no clear separation of urban and rural, and although proportions are comparable with other contemporary English populations, the Jewbury population is distinctive. This applies to low cranial vaults in males and relatively long faces (prominent maxillae) and high orbits in both sexes, and is especially apparent in comparison with Fishergate and St Helen-on-the-Walls. There were also differences in the curvature at the back of the skull, the nasal aperture and the palate. The Jewbury skulls also show distinctive discontinuous traits, like a high proportion of females with a metopic suture and of males with a low frequency of epipteric bones. All of this may have been brought about by a closed gene pool through the cultural or religious isolation of marriages only between Jews.

With regard to stature, Jewbury males were significantly shorter than their contemporaries, being 167.4cm as against 170.9cm for Fishergate, 169.3cm for St Helen-on-the-Walls and 169-171.6cm for other medieval English. Religious isolation and genetics may have been responsible for this difference too. Otherwise in medieval Yorkshire, there was low variation between rural and urban populations.

There was no sign at Jewbury of weight and other stresses in the limbs in the form of long-bone flattening (platymeria and platycnemia), although these occurred in other Yorkshire populations, urban and rural, with Wharram Percy showing the highest levels.

Morbidity and pathology. Sickliness can be related to all sorts of factors, such as adverse diet, high population densities, detrimental working conditions and polluted water. Thus there is evidence from the fish remains that the quality of the river water in York deteriorated between Roman and Medieval times, a factor which could have led to increased parasitism and disease. Pitting on the inside of the frontal plate of the orbit (or orbital cribra) occurred in 22% of the Jewbury population, due to one or several causes such as anaemia from metabolic and nutritional disease, iron deficiency or meningitis. In this, both Jewbury and Fishergate displayed low values compared with a large pooled English medieval series, while Wharram Percy displayed a high level, suggesting deprivation and a lower level of health. There were three possible cases of rickets and six tumour-like growths. Infections included many with periostitis (inflammation damage to the outer surface of the bone), suggestive of syphilis, leprosy or smallpox, although the aetiology of this condition is complex; its rate was lower at Jewbury than in the non-Jewish populations. Tuberculosis was definitely present in six cases and sinusitis in 31%. Twenty-seven skeletons had injuries, some deliberate and some showing no signs of healing; so there were violent deaths. One young woman, c15-20yrs, was hacked around the head, one blow removing her left ear, others almost decapitating her. There was an example of possible surgery in the treatment of a cranial injury. The number of healed long-bone fractures was low although with a puzzling high fibula percentage. Joint disease (arthropathy) was mostly of the knee with, in 152 such joints, 64% mild, 26% moderate and 9% severe; it was also in some vertebrae. There were two cases of biparietal thinning, one of Paget's disease and one of polio. Congenital pathologies included an adult female with severe dysplasia (abnormal growth) of the hips, 6 adults with abnormalities of cranial shape, 4 with sternal foramina, and 3 with vertebral union. But in general, the Jewbury population were a healthy lot - at least for the Middle Ages.

Teeth. Caries levels varied considerably, while the relatively high abscess frequency may be related to attrition and pulp exposure as well as caries. In spite of numbers of alveolar abscesses, ante-mortem tooth loss, pulpal exposures, malocclusion, abundant calculus and periodontal disease, frequencies were similar to other populations for the same period in the area. There were features however, such as the site specificity and type of caries and the prevalence of different types of malocclusion, which suggest distinctive facial conformations like large palatal breadth and certain patterns of disease.

KM Dobney has made a novel approach to ancient diet through a study of dental calculus: 'Within the calcified matrix of dental calculus lies a remarkable record of past oral ecology'. There were included pollen grains, plant strengthening vessels and phytoliths, mostly of cereals. There was also micro-banding of calcified and non-calcified materials, including plant tissue, highly calcified material, calcified masses of micro-organisms and microscopic lines. Incrementally banded calcification over a wide front represents rhythmic phases in the oral environment of secretions or temperature changes and the activities there of micro-organisms which could be clearly seen. The increments may be daily and reflect adherence to 'a very specific and orderly regime'. In one case the very last growth of bacteria before death was there.

Burial practice

Although somewhat diluted in towns, there was still some complete lay knowledge about processes of life **(p. 126)**. This is seen no less in burial practice than in other areas, with relationships between patterns and structures in living communities being translated into spatial and grave structures in the cemeteries. Especially this was through the expressive order. Kin and friends involved in the mortuary and burial process as well as the professionals who looked after the cemeteries and carried out the funerary business expressed their own inter-relationships through the dead.

These may have been played out in, for example, something as insignificant as what people looked like. Physiognomy, with all its trappings of prejudice, was a common, if often unspoken, communicational referent. Indeed, the significance of the face goes right back to the female figurines of the Ice Age, which deliberately lacked all details of it, and it is seen in the vogue for facial reconstructions from ancient skulls, even of *Homo erectus*, right up to today. People may have been prescribed particular rites, trappings and locations of burial just on the basis of their appearance if this was significant in the interrelations of those involved in the mortuary business. And if this were so, how much more likely was it that particular head shapes, statures, states of health, swollen gums, festering teeth, and scars and gashes, not to mention severed ears and heads, would have leant themselves to a similar response. We cannot keep separate the 'environmental evidence' of sanitary conditions and hygiene, the demographic parameters of age, sex, physique and health, on the one hand and the structure of the cemeteries and funerary practice in terms of these on the other.

First-burials were important to the future style of the cemetery, although there were differences of purpose in the different traditions. At Jewbury there was the explicit intention of creating a cemetery, and the first burial was placed in relation to others since he or she was buried with the plan and orientation of a future cemetery in mind. This was in the awareness of the person who dug the grave. That single person, imbued with deep Jewish traditions, working in ground which had been bought by the Jews, and outside but in sight of the city walls, had the plan of the future cemetery in mind. The first burials in the Christian cemeteries may have been more to do with the sanctification of a monastery or church, as with the enshrouded youth at Fishergate, than the beginnings of a cemetery *per se*, although this is perhaps a dangerous dichotomy.

Thus for subsequent burials we might suppose there were more possibilities for the establishment of complex relationships in the Christian than the Jewish cemeteries, where the architecture of church and liturgy acted as reflectors. But this might be to underestimate the complexities that can be introduced by kinship structures within the Jewish cemetery and even by mental ones. Groupings of related individuals in both traditions, Christian and Jewish, suggest a desire for close kin or similar professions to be buried as a group. This was known about, it was perpetuated in ceremony and prayer, it endowed the areas with further meaning, and it reflected back onto those groups in life. Then, meaning could be modified by the burial of a diversity of groups together. Females were placed around the periphery of, but not separate from, the monastic population; monastic retainers and their families were situated within the lay population; while family groupings in areas used by the wealthier members of the community and benefactors were closer than they were elsewhere. But this too enhanced the meanings of certain other areas where such dilution did not occur.

As the cemeteries grew there was the additional effect of their entirety. The Jewish cemetery was laid out without associated buildings and was seen as a cemetery with a future from the start. Being more uniform than the Christian cemeteries in terms of burial type and position, and more organised in terms of orientation, spacing and the care taken not to disturb previous burials, it reflected an organised and formal world. This may have been related variously to the precarious position of the Jews in England at this time as a persecuted minority, or it may have been a trait of Judaism *per se*, or perhaps it was a feature of religious orthodoxy in general. In York, it translated into everyday life in rigid eating patterns as seen in the regular layerings of dental calculus. And we might have expected even more order but the York Jews were preparing for expulsion and their population was reducing in the last few decades of their time in the city, eroding the importance of burial over everyday survival and planning for a future elsewhere. For the Christian cemeteries, continued use and remodelling and a not so rigid attitude to breaking into older burials meant that there was much reworking of burials and redeposition of bone in charnel deposits. We would like to know more about these, where they were and how they might have related to the perception of the various areas of the cemeteries, for they add another dimension of meaning. Nor was meaning static. Religious tastes and opportunities in terms of the importance and sanctity of particular monastic houses could change. So could dietary ones. A better standard of life could lead to poorer health if it became increasingly based on sugary foods, and so the perception of particular areas of the cemetery might change too. Buried bodies were also moved.

Further butchery

Three sites allow us to take a final look at bones, again based on the work of O'Connor. At Skeldergate (**83**), from a pit of the late eleventh and twelfth centuries, there were mainly cattle, the bones being waste from primary and secondary butchery; some carcasses were butchered as sides; most animals were between one and three years. From its systematic nature this was clearly commercial, while the sheep and pigs bones looked more like domestic waste. Another assemblage included goat and cattle horncores and suggested hornworking, although tannery or butchery are possibilities. Of the 50 goat horncores, only one had knife marks so the horn could have been removed by soaking them to rot the tissue between the horn itself and the core. Seven sheep mandibles were from animals in prime productivity, not 'elderly rejects from a wool flock'. So from this one small area there were bones from three origins, commercial butchery, domestic activity and craft.

From the same area, an early fifteenth-century cess-pit contained mainly sheep derived from a kitchen. The bones were mostly metapodials (ankles), perhaps the residues of skin processing, and the lack of cut marks suggests butchery with a knife rather than, as with the cattle, a cleaver. There were also bones of at least 5 cats, some dogs, cattle, pigs, rabbits, brown hare, fallow deer and black rats. There were 10 domestic fowl carcasses, and bones of goose, game birds and fish.

At Tanner Row and Rougier St (**83**), after the fourth century buildings had gone out of use (**p. 120**) there was little activity until the later Anglo-Scandinavian and Norman periods. Deposits contained plants likely to have been used in dyeing; there were different weed floras from those of the Roman period; and in the later Middle Ages generally, there was a resurgence of insects able to live in moderately clean conditions. Grain beetles were absent. Medieval garden-loams were cut into by pits of the twelfth and thirteenth centuries which were rich in human faeces as indicated by nematode eggs and worms, and with crushed herring and eel vertebrae, wheat/rye bran and corncockle seed fragments, and moss pads, all typical of faecal deposits.

Bones were mainly cattle, reflecting a dependence on beef, with some sheep and fewer pigs; horse and goat meat may also have been eaten, while fish added variety. There were also cats and dogs. One pit contained numerous cattle horncores and six of goat, a feature noted elsewhere in York at this time and probably the waste from artefact manufacture such as for knife-handles and rings. Another deposit was of secondary butchery waste with bones from the best parts of the carcass. The cattle were nearly all 3-4yrs old or more at death, in their prime as suppliers of haulage and milk but past their best as suppliers of tender beef. Animals were used as a multi-purpose resource and the city had no centralised beef or dairy industry at this time. The sheep were predominantly adult, but not particularly old, probably reflecting use for wool and manuring arable fields. There was abundant cod. Wild birds included guillemot and razorbill, probably from

Flamborough Head. Raven and black rat were present during a period of stone-robbing when the site may have been a run-down haunt of scavengers. Frog and water-vole indicate standing water in many of the pits.

Red squirrel (*Sciurus vulgaris*) is represented only by foot bones, as is the case for all other sites where this species occurs in medieval York; at the Bedern in a fourteenth-century pit, there were hundreds of them. So they were skinning red squirrels. These and other small fur-bearers like stoat (*Mustela erminea*) may have been used for their skins to wear as flea-furs. This was a practice in fifteenth-century Europe where flea-furs of squirrel, sable, ferret, weasel and ermine were worn around the neck and shoulders to attract fleas, when they were then shaken out. The Dukes of Burgundy replaced the eyes of their flea-furs with rubies and the feet with gilded claws. My grandmother had several fox furs in a chest of drawers which we used for dressing up with; but they were never called flea-furs.

In the early eighteenth century at Walmgate, on the east side of the River Foss in an industrial suburb (**83**), some pits were filled largely with sheep bone. The majority were mature and industrial waste from sheepskin preparation as shown by the predominance of metapodials and phalanges, with secondary use of proximal metatarsals for boneworking. There was a skeleton of a dog like a border collie, with a relatively long, slender muzzle.

These bone assemblages, showing the business of slaughter and butchery, the various uses of the animals and the disposal of their bones, are a part of the urban ecology, and there was a wide variety of activities; it sometimes seems that every assemblage is different. There were close associations between certain crafts or industries, such as tanning, glue manufacture and horn-working. Certain areas of the town, too, entailed a crossing over in the way in which meat was distributed. The monastery at Fishergate may have had contacts and meat supplies in the rural hinterland which were quite independent of the city, for example in its own granges, but there was almost certainly contact and exchange once the animals or meat came in. If, on the other hand, all or part of the monastic supplies came from the town, there would have been quite complex relationships. Certainly the bones from the site show a similarity with the city as a whole although with less diversity. Disposal of bone and offal from the monastery, too, was probably organised and independent, but some by-products like pigs' trotters or sheeps' feet may have been distributed to poor people.

12 Localities: the future

Archaeology has abundant data, with time resolutions from the more or less instantaneous to the scale of generations and longer, and much of them about the intimacies of every-day life. General aims should be to understand how people did things and why, rather than where and when. Temporo-spatial patternings — from the big units of archaeology to the smallest activity area in a room — have origins and influences which extend beyond their more obvious boundaries, and this makes them difficult to identify and leads one to suspect that they may not have existed.

Our approaches should be at the level of individual and community interactions. It is true, big spatio-temporal units of cultural identity and land may have been known about and have been a part of the understanding of how communities worked, as too may have been secular changes in things like climate and technology. And in this, our privileged position of being able to recognise these groupings *can* be useful in explaining what went on in the past. But we must study, too, *how* these groupings actually worked.

Interactions took place through the medium of the biophysical environment or events. Perception was important because it was through this that the biophysical environment was constituted. No artefact, like a woodland clearing, or no act, like a butchery, was ever seen in the same way more than once. Especially, a lot of effort was spent in establishing relations which were not obviously beneficial to the practicalities of a situation, and which, as the expressive order, could be responsible for how things were done and how they turned out. Nor was the form of an artefact or act the result of just its perception some way back in time. The steps in any process — the creation of a clearing or the butchery of an animal — were each as much artefacts as our idea of the finished clearing or butchery, and as such were just as prone to being modified. And I have hardly begun to explore the role of individual feelings in all this which Renato Rosaldo and Nadia Seremetakis have brought to us so poignantly.

Among the best materials for studying these interactions are animal bones because they are so abundant and reflect processes of everyday life. They reflect time and space well beyond the arena of the individual bones, after the butchery and before it. You can see this in the Tristan scene **(p. 14)**. At once this is about the details of butchery and the differences in this between cultures. But we are seeing, too, a reflection of deeper structures which separate the two cultures, while at the other extreme the whole scene may not really be about a hunt and butchery at all but the exploration and establishment of relationships. And this is being done too, not through the formality of ritual, but through 'ritualisation' — performance in the 'flux and contingency of everyday events' using the terminology of Seremetakis. So at another level it is about the personal joy and pride of

Tristan in demonstrating his skills and knowledge, and his behavioural quirks with his hair; and it is about the personal amazement of the huntsmen in witnessing them — although you can imagine some of the men thinking Tristan irksome (to put it politely). And, too, it is a small adventure in itself and a scene or prelude to a long love-story. Even in the distribution of the butchered parts, Tristan explains how to present the carcass at the court of King Mark: 'Convey the head in your hands, and take your present to court with all appropriate ceremony: this will enhance you as courtiers. You know yourselves how a hart must be presented. Present it in the approved manner!' And in fact use of a carcass and further distribution of its bits can extend over years, and be by people who had no part in the original slaughter. The whole business of animal and carcass interactions was complex, intimate and common: it took place all the time and practically everybody was involved.

You might say that other activities would also fit the bill, but there are objections. Human burial, while allowing the expression and development of the deepest personal feelings, is too focused on individuals, too specialised in its practitioners and too restricted in its archaeology to be of general relevance. With stone- and metal-working, although there is often clear usage of raw material extraction and artefact manufacture as agencies of the human expressive order, there is too much specialisation, and there is too little common interaction. Plant use lacks the element of destroying sentient beings. We worry about the rain forests not because of the trees *per se* but because of the effects on *our* atmosphere.

We worry about animals, or say we do, because of the animals themselves. And there is the key ingredient of slaughter. It is this, along with its mundaneness, that is so significant in the relationship with animals and which is found in no other arena of public life. We have in animal/human relationships something which goes on all the time, which interacts at a whole range of spatial and progressional scales, and in which all members of the community are involved, but which at the same time has just that degree of awfulness and specialism to allow the creation of oppositions of abhorrence and need, guilt and necessity, which are important for cementing communities and their lives.

Even today people engage more with butchers than with any other kind of shopkeeper, especially calling him (if the butcher is a him) by his first name. It is done in a particular way and it is almost always women of middle age who do it — not the younger or older women, and not the men. And the butchers themselves are pleased with this although they try not to show it. Why this should be is unclear: it may relate to biology, or to family values, or to some sort of personification of the purchases which is then transmitted to the table; it may be to do more with expressions of deep gender meaning than with the gender of the individuals themselves. This is not relevant here. What *is* relevant is that it is a clear example of fine behavioural mutualism in a very specific context and which is at the feather edge of maintaining and changing the more practical interactions that take place in these shops and among the people who are involved in them.

There really is a colossal amount of material, and bones have been at the centre of key issues in the development of archaeology. They launched the antiquity of the subject in the eighteenth century in their associations with stone tools. They were at the heart of Lewis Binford's seminal studies of middle range theory in the 1960s. They are playing a large part in the establishment of post-processualism in their role as mediators of human agency in the structured depositions in pits, ditches and tombs of the agricultural communities of prehistory. In urban archaeology they allow the articulation of the complex relationships between monasteries, the town communities and the farms and villages of the countryside to be played out, and are crucial in the identification of the economic and civic status of the towns themselves. In rural communities they enable us to look at the interface between perceptions of settlements and wilderness and, in the contacts with towns, how these might be transmitted into urban life. Microwear studies on teeth can tell us what sort of food the animals had been eating. And the bones are at the forefront of the very recent studies of chemical and biomolecular assays which can indicate not only the feeding environments of the animals but their genetic relationships as well. Would it not be marvellous to identify the farms where the cattle were reared so that we could know the places they went through as they came into the cities in their long journey from the fields?

Probably some dogs came too.

Glossary

Where a word is explained clearly in the text it is not included in the glossary.

alluviation The processes which lay down alluvium.

alluvium Any kind of river deposit, but often specifically fine loams formed by overbank flooding.

AMS dates Radiocarbon dates obtained by accelerator mass spectrometry which counts C-14 atoms rather than radioactivity, and can thus be used on very small samples.

argillic Clayey, usually with reference to soil texture.

Bayesian calibration The conversion of raw C-14 dates to calendrical ones using statistics which take into account the expected age of the materials being dated and the archaeological context. (For further details, see: CE Buck *et al*. 1996. *Bayesian approach to interpreting archaeological data*. John Wiley & Sons.)

biophysical environment That part of the environment relating to factors like climate and vegetation.

blanket peat Peat which covers great areas of land, usually in oceanic regions and is a response to high rainfall, as opposed to raised bogs which are of topographical origin **(p. 23)**.

bloodstone A hard, green silica-based rock, like chalcedony, with red spots.

bloom-smithing An intermediate stage in the production of iron from ore; the production of blooms.

Bos The generic name for cattle.

Boulder clay A deposit of clay and stones laid down by glaciers and ice-sheets; sometimes called 'till'.

calcareous granules Excretory products of wireworms, earthworms and molluscs; they often survive well in the soil and can be useful indicators of the activities of these animals **(p. 127)**.

carr woods Woods growing on peat, often of alder, willow or birch, and which are managed for their timber **(p. 95)**.

causewayed camps Embanked enclosures of the fourth and third millennia BC.

Chenopodiaceae Plants like goosefoot, fat hen and good King Henry which occur in waste ground, marsh or steppe.

colluvium Deposits laid down by subaerial (i.e. over land) processes, usually down slopes, such as ploughwash and cold-climate solifluxion materials.

coracoid A bony process at the base of the scapula (shoulder blade) close to the articulation with the humerus.

cord-rig Cultivation traces in the form of parallel closely-set ridges, 1.4m apart, done with an ard and usually prehistoric or Roman (Topping 1989).

cursuses Monumental linear earthworks consisting of two parallel banks and ditches, usually of the fourth and third millennia BC.

decachiliad A period of 10,000 years. For example, the second decachiliad is the period from 8000 to 18,000 BC.

diachronous Events taking place at different times, usually referring to similar events which might be thought to be synchronous because of their similarity but which are not.

discontinuous skeletal traits Traits which are absolute, like presence or absence of a certain bone (e.g. epipteric bones and metopic suture), and which do not merge into each other, as for example with stature or long-bone flattening and which are continuous traits.

eburnated Referring to bone surface which has been hardened and polished through localised and excessive use.

ecotonal Referring to areas, or **ecotones**, between two major ecosystems, as with the wetland habitats between lake and dryland.

environmental archaeology The study of the environments of past humans especially in archaeological contexts **(p. 5)**.

epiphyses The ends of bones, usually bearing articular surfaces, which remain unfused until adulthood.

epipteric bones An unusual condition, probably congenital, where there are small extra bones in the side of the skull.

fire-setting The quarrying of ores and stone by fracturing the rock-face with fire.

fluviatile Referring to river processes or environments.

Foraminifera Small, unicellular animals of the phylum Protozoa which secrete a hard calcareous test.

founder effect A situation where populations take on extreme characteristics because of derivation from a very few founder individuals.

gleys Soils which are semi- or totally waterlogged, and often grey or orange-mottled in colour.

glume One of the straw-like outer scales enclosing grass and cereal seeds.

Greensand A geological formation, occurring especially in the south and east of England.

head-dyke In upland farms, the wall between the enclosed farmland and the unenclosed grazing and peat.

hexaploid Refers to particular genetic forms of plant, especially cereals, which have six times the basic chromosome count in the cell nucleus.

hydrosere The succession of ecological communities from open water to dry land or raised bog **(pp. 23 and 44)**.

infield In upland farms, the most intensively worked land, usually nearest the settlement.

interfluves The area between two rivers, usually the watershed ridges.

isostasy, isostatic Referring to the raising and lowering of land in relation to the sea, usually in response to the melting or formation of ice-sheets **(p. 47) (31)**.

lagg The area between a bog and the dryland, often extremely wet and difficult to cross.

launder A wooden trough for conveying water.

maxillae The bones of the face in which the upper teeth are set.

metapodials Ankle bones, including metacarpals in front legs and metatarsals in the hind ones.

micromorphology The study of microscopic soil structure **(pp. 37 and 127)**.

milt The spleen.

monadnocks Rocky outcrops, similar to tors, of blue-stone or other volcanic rocks, specifically in the Preseli Hills **(48, 49)**.

multivariate analysis Statistical methods for dealing with large quantities of data where there are more than two variables.

narrow rig See cord rig.

nematodes Internal parasitic worms of pigs and humans, including *Ascaris* spp. and *Trichuris* spp.

nitrophile, nitrophilous Refers to plants which live in organic-rich habitats, especially around human settlements.

palynology The study of vegetational and climate history through the use of pollen grains from lake sediments and peat bogs.

periderm The coat or test of cereal grains, often preserved in bran because of its hardness.

phalanges Fingers and toes, especially the bones.

phenomenology The (study of) experiences of individuals through the senses **(p. 5)**; the appearance which anything makes to our consciousness as opposed to what it is itself; the philosophy of Edmund Husserl (1859-1938).

physiognomy The art of judging character by appearances, especially from the face.

phytoliths Microscopic silica inclusions in plant cells, often preserved in soils and dental calculus.

podzols Soils in which iron and other nutrients have been washed out of the upper horizons, often forming a pan lower down.

proximal The bone or end of a bone nearest to the spine.

pyrotechnology The technology of using and controlling fire, as in metalworking, pottery manufacture, cooking and cremation.

reeves Boundary earthworks of the third millennium BC, especially in Dartmoor **(p. 29)**.

rhyolite A very fine-grained igneous rock, formed by volcanic activity, and which is easily flaked.

sarsen A hard, crystalline, silica or quartzite rock which occurs as large blocks on the surface of chalk areas **(57)**.

souterrains Underground stone built galleries of the first millennium BC and later, usually associated with settlements.

spacing behaviour The distribution of animals in relation to each other.

stable isotope analysis In the context of bone, this is a techique for identifying different sorts of diet, especially the contrast between marine- and land-based; the analysis of different forms of non-radioactive carbon and oxygen.

stagno-soils Soils in which there is a significant peaty component.

synanthropes, synathropous species Forms and species of plants and animals which thrive in and are specially adapted to human habitations.

taphonomy The (study of) the processes which result in the burial and preservation of ancient life; originally applied to animal remains, it is now used more widely in archaeology for all burial processes.

till See 'boulder clay'.

tranchet flake A flake removed from a stone tool, usually from its working end and often obliquely to the long axis, in order to sharpen it.

wear analysis The examination of the edges and surfaces of teeth and tools for traces of specific kinds of use.

References

Arch. J. = Archaeological Journal
BAR = British Archaeological Reports
CBA = Council for British Archaeology
CUP = Cambridge University Press
EUP = Edinburgh University Press
JAS = Journal of Archaeological Science
PPS = Proceedings of the Prehistoric Society
PSAS = Proceedings of the Society of Antiquaries of Scotland

History of human environments in the British Isles

Caseldine A 1990. *Environmental archaeology in Wales*. St David's University College
    Lampeter.
Chambers FM (ed.) 1993. *Climate change and human impact on the landscape*. Chapman &
    Hall.
Edwards K & Ralston I (eds) 1996. *Environmental archaeology of Scotland*. EUP.
Evans JG 1975. *The environment of early man in the British Isles*. Paul Elek.
Jones RL & Keen DH 1993. *Pleistocene environments in the British Isles*. Chapman & Hall.
F Mitchell 1986. *Reading the Irish landscape*. Country House.
Preece RJ (ed.) 1995. *Island Britain: a Quaternary perspective*. Geological Society.
Simmons IG & Tooley MJ (eds) 1981. *The environment in British prehistory*. Duckworth.

For localities

Dickens P 1990. *Urban sociology: society, locality and human nature*. Harvester, Wheatsheaf.
Dobres M-A 1995. Gender and prehistoric technology: on the social agency of technical
    strategies. *World Archaeology* 27, 25-49.
Goffman E 1963. *Behaviour in public places*. Free Press.
Goffman E 1969. *The presentation of self in everyday life*. Penguin Books.

Sources of the case studies

1   Some early people
Callow P & Cornford JM (eds) 1986. *La Cotte de St. Brelade 1961-1978: excavations by CBM*
    McBurney. Geo Books.
Conway B *et al.* 1996. *Excavations at Barnfield Pit, Swanscombe, 1968-72*. British Museum.
Cranshaw S 1983. *Handaxes and cleavers: selected English Acheulian industries*. BAR.
Gamble C 1986. *The Palaeolithic settlement of Europe*. CUP.
Roberts MB *et al.* 1997. Boxgrove, West Sussex: rescue excavations of a Lower Palaeolithic
    landsurface. *PPS* 63, 303-58.
Singer R *et al.* 1973. Excavation of the Clactonian industry at the golf course,
    Clacton-on-Sea, Essex. *PPS* 39, 6-74.
2   To the end of the Ice Age
Aldhouse-Green S *et al.* 1995. Coygan Cave, Laugharne, South Wales. *PPS* 61, 37-79.
Barton N 1997. *Stone Age Britain*. Batsford.
Green S 1986. Excavations at Little Hoyle (Longbury Bank), Wales. *In* DA Roe (ed.),
    Studies in the Upper Palaeolithic of Britain and northwest Europe. BAR; pp.99-119.
Housley RA *et al.* 1997. Radiocarbon evidence for the Lateglacial recolonisation of Europe.
    PPS 63, 25-54.

3   Fforest Fawr, Dartmoor and the East Anglian fen-edge

Balaam ND *et al*. 1982. The Shaugh Moor project: fourth report. *PPS* 48, 203-78.

Barton RNE *et al*. 1995. Persistent places in the Mesolithic landscape. *PPS* 61, 81-116.

Caseldine C & Hatton J 1993. The development of high moorland on Dartmoor. *In* FM Chambers (ed.), *Climate change and human impact on the landscape*. Chapman & Hall; pp.119-31.

French CAI 1988. Further aspects of the buried prehistoric soils in the fen margin north east of Peterborough. *In* P Murphy & C French (eds), *The exploitation of wetlands*. BAR; pp.193-211.

French CAI 1990. Neolithic soils, middens and alluvium in the lower Welland Valley. *Oxford Journal of Archaeology* 9, 305-11.

French CAI *et al*. 1992. Archaeology and palaeochannels in the lower Welland and Nene Valleys. *In* S Needham & MG Macklin (eds), *Alluvial archaeology in Britain*. Oxbow; pp.169-76.

Moore PD 1993. The origin of blanket mire, revisited. *In* FM Chambers (ed.), *Climate change and human impact on the landscape*. Chapman & Hall; pp.217-24.

Pryor F 1996. Sheep, stockyards and field systems. *Antiquity* 70, 313-24.

Simmons IG *et al*. 1983. A further pollen analytical study of the Blacklane peat section on Dartmoor, England. *New Phytologist* 94, 655-67.

Smith AG & Cloutman EW 1988. Reconstruction of Holocene vegetation history in three dimensions at Waun-Fignen-Felen. *Philosophical Transactions of the Royal Society* B322, 159-219.

Smith AG *et al*. 1989. Mesolithic and Neolithic activity and environmental impact on the south-east fen-edge in Cambridgeshire. *PPS* 55, 207-49.

Smith K *et al*. 1981. The Shaugh Moor project: third report. *PPS* 47, 205-73.

4   North-east Ireland to the Shetlands

Armit I 1992. *The later prehistory of the Western Isles of Scotland*. BAR.

Davidson DA *et al*. 1986. The formation of farm mounds on the island of Sanday, Orkney. *Geoarchaeology* 1, 45-60.

Davidson DA & Simpson IA 1984. The formation of deep topsoils in Orkney. *Earth Surface Processes and Landforms* 9, 75-81.

Dockrill SJ & Simpson IA 1994. The identification of prehistoric anthropogenic soils in the Northern Isles. *Archaeological Prospection* 1, 75-92.

Dodgshon RA 1994. Budgeting for survival. *In* S Foster & TC Smout (eds), *The history of soils and field systems*. Scottish Cultural Press; pp.83-93.

Fojut N 1982. Towards a geography of Shetland brochs. *Glasgow Archaeological Journal* 9, 39-59.

Hingley R 1996. Ancestors and identity in the later prehistory of Atlantic Scotland. *World Archaeology* 28, 231-43.

Lowe C 1998. *Coastal erosion and the archaeological assessment of an eroding shoreline at St Boniface Church, Papa Westray, Orkney*. Sutton.

Mellars P 1987. *Excavations on Oronsay*. EUP.

Parker Pearson M *et al*. 1996. Brochs and Iron Age society. *Antiquity* 70, 57-67.

Pollard T & Morrison A (eds) 1996, *The early prehistory of Scotland*. EUP.

Sharples N & Parker Pearson M 1997. Why were brochs built? *In* A Gwilt & C Haselgrove (eds), *Reconstructing Iron Age societies*. Oxbow; pp.254-65.

Singh G & Smith AG 1973. Post-glacial vegetational history in Lecale, Co. Down. *Proceedings of the Royal Irish Academy* B, 73, 1-51.

5   Inorganic raw materials

Crew P 1986. Bryn y Castell hillfort. *In* BG Scott & H Cleere (eds), *The crafts of the blacksmith*. UISPP; pp.91-100.

Dutton A & Fasham PJ 1994. Prehistoric copper mining on the Great Orme, Llandudno, Gwynedd. *PPS* 60, 245-86.

Hanworth R & Tomalin DJ 1977. *Brooklands, Weybridge*. Surrey Archaeological Society.

Hingley R 1997. Iron, ironworking and regeneration. *In* A Gwilt & C Haselgrove (eds), *Reconstructing Iron Age societies*. Oxbow; pp.9-18.

Jackson DA & Ambrose TM 1978. Excavations at Wakerley, Northants, 1972-75. *Britannia* 9, 115-242.

Lewin J *et al.* 1977. Interactions between channel change and historic mining sediments. *In* KJ Gregory (ed.), *River channel changes*. John Wiley & Sons; pp.353-67.

Macklin MG *et al.* 1985. Early mining in Britain. *In* NRJ Fieller *et al.* (eds), *Palaeoenvironmental investigations*. BAR; pp.45-54.

Mighall TM & Chambers FM 1993. The environmental impact of prehistoric mining at Copa Hill, Cwmystwyth, Wales. *The Holocene* 3, 260-64.

Mighall TM & Chambers FM 1997. Early ironworking and its impact on the environment. *PPS* 63, 199-219.

O'Brien WF 1990. Prehistoric copper mining in south-west Ireland: the Mount Gabriel type mines. *PPS* 56, 269-90.

Russell M 1997. NEO-'Realism?': an alternative look at the Neolithic chalkland database of Sussex. *In* P Topping (ed.), *Neolithic landscapes*. Oxbow; pp.69-76.

Taylor KJ 1996. The rough and the smooth. *In* T Pollard & A Morrison (eds), *The early prehistory of Scotland*. EUP; pp.225-36.

Timberlake S 1993. Copa Hill, Cwmystwyth. *Archaeology in Wales* 33, 54-55.

Williams TM 1991. A sedimentary record of the deposition of heavy metals and magnetic oxides in the Loch Dee basin, Galloway, Scotland, since c. AD 1500. *The Holocene* 1, 142-50.

6   The Cheviot Hills and the Milfield Basin

Richards C 1996. Henges and water. *Journal of Material Culture* 1, 313-36.

Tipping R 1992. The determination of cause in the generation of major prehistoric valley fills in the Cheviot Hills. *In* S Needham & MG Macklin (eds), *Alluvial archaeology in Britain*. Oxbow; pp.111-21.

Tipping R 1996. The Neolithic landscapes of the Cheviot Hills and hinterland. *Northern Archaeology* 13/14, 17-33.

Topping P 1989. Early cultivation in Northumberland and the Borders. *PPS* 55, 161-79.

Topping P 1997. Different realities. *In* P Topping (ed.), *Neolithic landscapes*. Oxbow; pp.113-23.

7   The River Tyne and Hadrian's Wall

Barber KE *et al.* 1994. A sensitive high-resolution record of late Holocene climatic change from a raised bog in northern England. *The Holocene* 4, 198-205.

Barber KE *et al.* 1993. Climatic change and human impact during the late Holocene in northern Britain. *In* FM Chambers (ed.), *Climate change and human impact on the landscape*. Chapman & Hall; pp.225-36.

Chambers FM *et al.* 1997. A 5500-year proxy-climate and vegetation record from blanket mire at Talla Moss, Borders, Scotland. *The Holocene* 7, 391-99.

Dumayne & Barber KE 1994. The impact of the Romans on the environment of northern England. *The Holocene* 4, 165-73.

Ferrell G 1997. Space and society in the Iron Age of north-east England. *In* A Gwilt & C Haselgrove (eds), *Reconstructing Iron Age societies*. Oxbow; pp.228-38.

Manning A *et al.* 1997. Roman impact on the environment at Hadrian's Wall. *The Holocene* 7, 175-86.

Macklin MG *et al.* 1992. Climatic and cultural signals in Holocene alluvial sequences. *In* S Needham & MG Macklin (eds), *Alluvial archaeology in Britain*. Oxbow; pp.123-39.

McCarthy MR 1995. Archaeological and environmental evidence for the Roman impact on vegetation near Carlisle, Cumbria. *The Holocene* 5, 491-95.

Passmore DG *et al.* 1992. A Holocene alluvial sequence in the Lower Tyne Valley. *The Holocene* 2, 138-47.

Tipping R 1997. Pollen analysis and the impact of Rome on native agriculture around Hadrian's Wall. *In* A Gwilt & C Haselgrove (eds), *Reconstructing Iron Age societies: new approaches to the British Iron Age*. Oxbow; pp.239-47.

van der Veen M 1992. *Crop husbandry regimes*. Collis.

van der Veen M & O'Connor T 1998. The expansion of agricultural production in late Iron Age and Roman Britain. *In* J Bayley (ed.), *Science in archaeology*. English Heritage; pp.127-43.

8   Oppida
Bradley R 1971. A field survey of the Chichester entrenchments. *In* B Cunliffe, *Excavations at Fishbourne 1961-1969*. Society of Antiquaries; pp.17-36.
Collis J 1984. *Oppida: earliest towns north of the Alps*. University of Sheffield.
Haselgrove C & Millett M 1997. Verlamion reconsidered. *In* A Gwilt & C Haselgrove (eds), *Reconstructing Iron Age societies*. Oxbow; pp.282-96.
Haselgrove CC *et al*. 1990. Stanwick, North Yorkshire, part 3: excavations on earthworks sites 1981-86. *Arch. J.* 147, 37-90.
Hunn JR 1992. The Verulamium oppidum and its landscape in the Late Iron Age. *Arch. J.* 149, 39-68.
Neal DS *et al*. 1990. *Excavations of the Iron Age, Roman and medieval settlement at Gorhambury, St Albans*. English Heritage.
Stead IM & Rigby V 1989. *Verulamium: the King Harry Lane site*. English Heritage.
Woolf G 1993. Rethinking the oppida. *Oxford Journal of Archaeology* 12, 223-34.

9   Roman towns
Dickens P 1996. *Reconstructing nature*. Routledge.
Hall AR & Kenward HK 1990. *Environmental evidence from the Colonia*. CBA.
Hall AR *et al*. 1980. *Environmental evidence from Roman deposits in Skeldergate*. CBA.
Hall R 1996. *York*. Batsford.
Kenward HK *et al*. 1986. *Environmental evidence from a Roman well and Anglian pits in the Legionary Fortress*. CBA.
Kenward HK & Williams D 1979. *Biological evidence from the Roman warehouses in Coney Street*. CBA.
McCarthy MR 1990. *A Roman, Anglian and medieval site at Blackfriars Street, Carlisle*. Cumberland & Westmorland Archaeological and Antiquarian Society.
McCarthy MR 1991. *Roman waterlogged remains at Castle Street, Carlisle*. Cumberland and Westmorland Antiquarian & Archaeological Society.
McCarthy MR 1991. *The structural sequence and environmental remains from Castle Street, Carlisle*. Cumberland and Westmorland Antiquarian & Archaeological Society.
O'Connor TP 1984. *Selected groups of bones from Skeldergate and Walmgate*. CBA.
O'Connor TP 1988. *Bones from the General Accident site, Tanner Row*. CBA.

10   Dark-earth and Anglian and Anglo-Scandinavian York
Bond JM & O'Connor TP 1998. *Bones from medieval deposits at 16-22 Coppergate and other sites in York*. CBA.
Hall AR *et al*. 1983. *Environment and living conditions at two Anglo-Scandinavian sites*. CBA.
Hall R 1994. *Viking Age York*. Batsford.
Kenward HK & Hall AR 1995. *Biological evidence from 16-22 Coppergate*. CBA.
Macphail RI 1981. Soil and botanical studies of the 'dark earth'. *In* M Jones & G Dimbleby (eds), *The environment of man*. BAR; 309-31.
Macphail RI 1994. The re-working of urban stratigraphy by human and natural processes. *In* AR Hall & HK Kenward (eds), *Urban-rural connexions*. Oxbow; pp.13-43.
O'Connor TP 1989. *Bones from Anglo-Scandinavian levels at 16-22 Coppergate*. CBA.
O'Connor TP 1991. *Bones from 46-54 Fishergate*. CBA.
Seremetakis CN 1991. *The last word: women, death and divination in Inner Mani*. University of Chicago Press.

11   Medieval York
Brothwell D 1994. On the possibility of urban-rural contrasts in human population palaeobiology. *In* AR Hall & HK Kenward (eds), *Urban-rural connexions*. Oxbow; pp.129-36.
Dobney KM 1994. Study of the dental calculus. *In* JM Lilley *et al*. 1994.
Lilley JM *et al*. 1994. *The Jewish burial ground at Jewbury*. CBA.
Stroud G & Kemp RL 1993. *Cemeteries of the church and priory of St Andrew, Fishergate*. CBA.

12 Localities: the future
Rosaldo R 1993. *Culture and truth: the remaking of social analysis*. Routledge.

Index